10

minutes
to table

10

minutes
to table

Xanthe Clay

MITCHELL BEAZLEY

For Richard, of course

10 Minutes to Table
Xanthe Clay

An Hachette Livre UK Company
www.hachettelivre.co.uk

First published in Great Britain in 2009 by Mitchell Beazley
An imprint of Octopus Publishing Group Ltd,
2–4 Heron Quays, London E14 4JP
www.octopusbooks.co.uk

As seen on Telegraph TV

Telegraph TV

ISBN   978 1 84533 4956

A CIP record for this book is available from the British Library

Commissioning Editor Rebecca Spry
Designers Pene Parker and Juliette Norsworthy
Photographer Chris Terry
Project Editor Georgina Atsiaris
Copy Editor Diona Gregory
Home Economist Sara Lewis
Stylist Isabel de Cordova
Production controller Lucy Carter
Proofreader Jo Murray
Indexer Diana LeCore

Set in Glypha LT

Printed and bound by Toppan Printing Company, China

Contents

Introduction   6

Meat   8

Birds   52

Fish   88

Veg   132

Fast ingredients   172

Basic rules for fast food   174

Index   175

We don't have time to cook. Or that's what the food manufacturers would like us to believe, with their slickly packaged ready dishes offering 'home cooked taste' or 'restaurant quality' without mess, or care, or trouble, or any of those normal parts of life.

But the truth is, if we have time to heat a ready meal, we've got time to cook. The minutes that soulless plastic tray of tired mush takes to heat through safely, are time enough to cook some proper food.

Not that it's always easy. After an exhausting day working few people want to spend ages at the stove. So, why bother? Because it tastes good, and it feels good, if only because there's often too little opportunity for creativity in a busy life.

Homemade food is real food, with none of the mysterious additives that a glance at a ready meal ingredients list reveals, or that lurk in a takeaway. It's also fresh. With a few honourable exceptions, mostly in the long, slow cooked casserole category, food does not taste better if it is made days, weeks even, in advance, as ready meals may be. Food does taste better cooked at home from real produce, fruit, vegetables, fish and meat, and it's better for you too.

The way to balance the time/food equation is to cook simple, easy dishes most days, the sort of stuff that can be thrown together from a few fresh ingredients. In this book I've given some ideas for exactly that.

I don't use a microwaves either, not because I have anything against them. They are great for heating milk or steaming vegetables. But watching a plate spin through a glass screen doesn't really seem like cooking to me. I like to engage with my food.

I've also avoided 'cheats', the kind that involve whipping up a clever casserole with a tin of mushroom soup. There are three main reasons for this. I don't want to send you schlepping round shops for a particular brand which is the only one that will work; they often contain doubtful ingredients; and on top of that they can give otherwise homemade food a shop-bought taste – and what's the point of that?

That's not to say that the odd preprepared supermarket standby won't creep in – a dollop of pesto sauce, a tub of stock, or a packet of garlicky cream cheese. But many chill-cabinet 'standbys' can be made by hand in a couple of minutes, less even. Try the homemade humuus on page 42 if you don't believe me. By and large, homemade food should be just that – homemade.

All of these recipes really can be cooked in ten minutes (or five minutes, for the five minute ones, obviously). If you don't believe me, log on to the website (www.telegraph.co.uk/food) and you can see it happening. The food is cooked in 'real time', that's to say with no cheating, no cuts, and absolutely no pre-preparation or behind the scenes help. It genuinely is carrier bag to plate in ten. I don't even get to rehearse in the studio.

That said I have, of course, now got quite practiced. So the first time you cook these recipes some may take longer than ten minutes. Don't be resentful. You'll get faster. And the point is, that none of the recipes, even if taken at a gentle jog rather than an all out sprint, should take longer than twenty minutes. There just isn't that much to do. So get in the kitchen, grab a pan and get cooking. Good food isn't complicated. It's easy.

Xanthe Clay

10 : Meat

minutes to table

Parmesan beef burger with tomato and balsamic relish and chips

A proper burger, a fat patty of decent mince, is a thing of joy and a gastronomic glory that can be made in less time than it takes to defrost a disc of 'non-specific meat product'. Parmesan makes the burger extra savoury, but if it seems a bit la-di-dah leave it out.

Serves 2

for the burgers:
300g (11oz) minced beef
hunk of Parmesan, big enough to grate 3 tbsp
small bunch of flat-leaf parsley, chopped
splash of soy sauce
2 ciabatta rolls
a few lettuce leaves
1 small red onion
for the tomato and balsamic relish:
3 ripe tomatoes
2 tbsp aged balsamic vinegar
1 tsp sugar (any kind will do)
1 tbsp tiny capers (optional)
for the chips:
1 huge potato (or 2 medium)
vegetable oil, for deep frying

1. Put the kettle on to boil. Heat a griddle or heavy frying pan until very hot. Flick a droplet of water on; if it sizzles and evaporates the pan's hot enough.

2. Cut the potatoes into pencil thin sticks. Cook in a pan of the boiling water for 1–2 minutes.

3. Meanwhile, heat the oil, 1.5cm (½ inch) deep, in a wide pan until shimmeringly hot.

4. Mix the beef with the grated Parmesan, parsley, salt, pepper and soy sauce. Shape into two patties and cook on the heated griddle or frying pan until cooked to your liking, turning once.

5. Drain the potatoes, dry on a tea towel and cook in the hot oil until golden and crisp. Scoop out the chips with a slotted spoon and drain on kitchen paper.

6. Roughly chop the tomatoes and put them in a small pan with the balsamic vinegar, sugar and a pinch of salt. Cook until the tomatoes are soft and the juices thicken. Stir in the capers, if using, taste and adjust the seasoning.

7. Halve the ciabatta rolls and toast them (or brown them on the griddle). Lay a few lettuce leaves on the two bottom halves and cut a thin onion ring for each. Top with the burgers, some relish and the top of the roll. Serve with the chips and any leftover relish.

Rare beef with radish, cress and pea salad

This is a summery favourite, good for lunch with brown bread.

Serves 2

110g (4oz) peas (fresh podded or frozen)
beef fillet (its size depends on how hungry you are, but about 110–225g/4–8oz)
1 tbsp cracked black pepper (buy ready-cracked pepper, or smash your own with
  a pestle and mortar)
small bunch of radishes
1 punnet of cress (or mustard and cress)
3 tbsp crème fraîche
lime wedges

1. Put the kettle on to boil. Heat a heavy frying pan or griddle until very hot and a droplet of
   water flicked onto it sizzles and evaporates.

2. Pod the peas if using fresh, then cook them briefly in a pan of well-salted boiling water until
   just tender. Drain and cool thoroughly under cold running water.

3. Roll the beef in the pepper. Cook the beef on the hot pan or griddle for about 30 seconds
   on each side. The heat should have penetrated about 0.5cm (¼ inch) into the meat on
   both sides.

4. Slice the radishes thinly and pile on a serving plate with the cress and peas. Slice the beef
   very thinly and arrange on top. Thin the crème fraîche slightly with water to a yoghurty
   consistency and trickle over the beef. Serve straight away, with lime wedges to squeeze
   over the top, and perhaps a small drizzle of olive oil.

A few minutes more: Boil some baby new potatoes and toss them in butter,
chopped chives and a bit of grated lime zest stolen from the lime wedges.
Serve alongside the salad.

Rose veal with cherry tomato sauce, thyme-scented polenta and spinach

Veal has an undeserved reputation for being cruel and unethical. In fact, pink British rose veal (as opposed to white veal) is produced to exemplary welfare standards. And because veal calves are an inevitable outcome of the dairy industry, if you eat cheese or drink milk, you really ought to eat veal. It's delicious, too.

Serves 2

200g (7oz) rose veal fillet
2 tbsp olive oil
250g (9oz) red and yellow cherry tomatoes
1 clove of garlic, peeled
½ teacupful of quick-cook '1 minute' polenta
few sprigs of lemon thyme
2 tbsp butter, plus 1 tsp butter
hunk of Parmesan, big enough to grate 3 tbsp
handful of spinach leaves, washed

1. Put the kettle on to boil and heat a heavy frying pan until very hot. Cut the veal into 1.5cm (½ inch) slices and season with salt and pepper. Add 1 tbsp oil to the frying pan and cook the veal for a minute or so on each side, until slightly pink in the middle.

2. Heat 1 tbsp oil in a shallow pan until hot. Cut the tomatoes in half. Slice the garlic thinly and add half to the pan, followed by the tomatoes. Cook gently (you don't want them to collapse) for 2 minutes.

3. Put the polenta in a pan with 2 teacupfuls of boiling water, the rest of the garlic, and a couple of sprigs of thyme. Simmer, stirring often, until thick. Stir in 1 tbsp butter and 3 tbsp grated Parmesan, plus the leaves from the rest of the thyme.

4. Stir 1 tbsp butter into the tomatoes. It will emulsify into a sauce, but don't let it boil from now on or it may split.

5. Melt 1 tsp butter in a large pan over a medium-high heat and add the spinach and a good pinch of salt. Stir just until wilted.

6. Serve the veal with the tomato sauce, polenta and wilted spinach.

A few minutes less: Dispense with the polenta and wilted spinach and have some good bread and a spinach salad instead.

Steak au poivre with parsnip chips

Parsnips can be used to make great fast chips and their sweetness is delicious with this peppery sauce. The thickness of the steak is more important than the weight here (140g/5oz is plenty for most people, but be guided by your hunger).

Serves 2

vegetable oil
2 fillet steaks, each about 2cm (¾ inch) thick
4 parsnips
2 tbsp brandy
large dollop of crème fraîche
1 tsp mixed peppercorns
bunch of watercress

1. Heat two heavy frying pans, the larger with 0.5cm (¼inch) oil until shimmeringly hot, the other empty until very hot and a droplet of water flicked on to it sizzles and evaporates.

2. Dry the steaks well with kitchen paper.

3. Add 1 tsp oil to the smaller pan and put the steaks in. Cook for about 2 minutes, until browned, then turn and cook on the other side until cooked the way you like them.

4. Meanwhile, peel the parsnips and halve them crossways. Cut the fat ends lengthways into four and the thin ends into two. Cook in the hot oil, turning every minute or so, until golden brown on all sides. Drain on kitchen paper and keep warm.

5. Remove the steaks from the pan and splash the brandy in, letting it bubble up and even flame if it wants to. Stir in the crème fraîche. Crush the peppercorns slightly in a pestle and mortar and add to the sauce. Stir well, letting it bubble and darken. Add 1 tbsp of water if it looks like it is curdling. Taste and season with salt.

6. Put the steaks on two plates, pour over the warm sauce and serve with the parsnips and a posy of watercress.

A few minutes less: Don't bother with the parsnip chips; instead, serve the steak with good bread, watercress and a bag of vegetable crisps warmed through in a low oven.

Calves' liver alla veneziana with beetroot purée and watercress

Liver gets a bad press, and if it's overcooked pig's liver – grey, tough and strong tasting – it probably deserves it. Calves' liver, lightly cooked so it is still pink inside, is another matter altogether. Try it with softly caramelized onions and a vivid red beetroot purée.

Serves 4

2 tbsp olive oil
3 tbsp unsalted butter
2 red onions
1 tsp honey
1 sage leaf
1 x 250g vacuum pack of cooked beetroot (choose the kind without vinegar)
250g (9oz) calves' liver, thinly sliced
3–4 tbsp red wine
few drops of balsamic vinegar
bunch of watercress or handful of frisée lettuce

1. Put the kettle on to boil. Heat 1 tbsp olive oil with 1 tbsp butter in a large, heavy frying pan on a medium-low heat.

2. Peel and grate the onions coarsely and add to the pan with a good pinch of salt, the honey and sage leaf. Cook, stirring occasionally.

3. Purée the beetroot with a hand blender. Heat through in a pan with 1 tbsp butter. Taste and season with salt and pepper.

4. In another large frying pan, heat 1 tbsp oil until shimmeringly hot. Add the liver to the pan, sprinkle with salt, and cook for 30–45 seconds on each side, until well browned but still just pink in the middle.

5. Add the wine to this pan and scrape the bottom of the pan with a wooden spoon to dislodge any browned bits. Add the remaining 1 tbsp butter and the vinegar.

6. Serve the liver with the onions, beetroot purée, wine sauce and a little watercress or frisée lettuce.

A few minutes less: Use a jar of caramelized onions, heated through gently, instead of cooking the onions from scratch. Bay Tree and Wiltshire Tracklements are both good brands.

Saltimbocca with green beans, polenta and Marsala gravy

Classically, this is done with veal, which can be hard to find even though British rose veal is ethically produced and delicious. Try Marks & Spencer, Waitrose or a good butcher. Pork makes a good alternative, as does a skinless chicken breast sliced in half horizontally, but do make sure they are cooked through.

Serves 2

2 rose veal steaks
2–4 sage leaves
4 slices of prosciutto
butter
½ x 500g block of ready-cooked polenta
1 clove of garlic, peeled
olive oil
generous handful of green beans
4 tbsp Marsala

1. Put the kettle on to boil. Heat a griddle pan and a heavy frying pan until hot.

2. Trim the veal steaks and bash them with a rolling pin to flatten slightly. Lay 1–2 sage leaves on each steak and wrap in prosciutto.

3. Melt a generous knob of butter, about 2 tbsp, in the hot frying pan and cook the veal for about 3 minutes on each side until browned and cooked through. Take out and keep warm.

4. Slice the polenta as thick as a finger. Crush the garlic and mix with 2 tbsp olive oil, then smear over the polenta. Cook on the hot griddle for 2–3 minutes on each side, until the slices are nicely browned.

5. Steam the beans until just done. Mix with a knob of butter, a pinch of salt and a grinding of black pepper.

6. Splash the Marsala into the hot veal pan, stirring vigorously as it bubbles up to make a sauce. Add a little water to the pan if it looks curdled. Taste and add seasoning and/or another knob of butter.

7. Arrange the veal, polenta and beans on two plates and pour over the Marsala gravy.

Polenta, prosciutto and green beans

This is comfort in a bowl for a chilly day. Instead of the prosciutto, you could eat the polenta with some grilled salmon or on its own. It's the food equivalent of a little black dress, perfect with everything.

Serves 2

generous handful of green beans
½ teacupful of quick-cook '1 minute' polenta
1 clove of garlic, peeled
hunk of Parmesan, big enough to grate 3 tbsp
1 tbsp butter
4 slices of prosciutto

1. Put the kettle on to boil. Pour a little boiling water in a small saucepan and bring back to the boil. Top and tail the beans and drop them in. Cover and leave to simmer until just cooked.

2. Put the polenta in a pan and add 2 teacupfuls of boiling water. Crush in the garlic and a fat pinch of salt and bring to simmering point, stirring occasionally.

3. When thick and creamy, grate in 3 tbsp Parmesan and stir in ½ tbsp butter, taste and check the seasoning.

4. Drain the beans and mix with the rest of the butter, a pinch of salt and a good grinding of black pepper.

5. Serve the polenta with the beans and the prosciutto tumbled beside it.

5
minutes
to table

Devilled kidneys on toast

Kidneys make me think of Victorian gentlemen's clubs and red velvet curtains, especially when cooked in this spicy sauce. They are absolutely delicious, as long as they aren't overcooked, which turns them rubbery: the middle should still be pink. A bonus is that they are still fantastically cheap, so snap them up now before the celebrity chefs discover them and the price soars.

Serves 2

1 tsp butter
6–8 lambs' kidneys
2 slices of good bread
1 tsp Worcestershire sauce
1 tbsp tomato purée
½ tsp English mustard
chilli sauce
½ lemon
small bunch of flat-leaf parsley

1. Put a large, heavy frying pan (one big enough to take the sliced kidneys in a single layer) on a high heat and add the butter.

2. Slice the kidneys into four lengthways, making four 'kidney-shaped' slices. There is a core that you could snip out with sharp, pointed kitchen scissors, but that will probably take you over the 5 minutes. They are easy to cut out as you eat, anyway.

3. Add the kidneys to the butter and cook for 30 seconds to 1 minute on each side, until they are lightly browned.

4. Meanwhile, put the bread on to toast.

5. Stir the Worcestershire sauce, tomato purée, mustard and a shake of chilli sauce into the pan of kidneys, and cook for a few seconds. Add a squeeze of lemon juice, taste and season with salt and freshly ground black pepper.

6. Put the toast onto two plates and pile on the kidneys and sauce. Snip over the parsley and serve straight away.

5
minutes
to table

Pork with sweet potato mash, mustard sauce and sizzling spring onions

Cut fairly thin, and cooked fast, pork steaks stay moist and tender – perfect with sweet potatoes, perfumed with Angostura bitters. A bottle of bitters seems expensive but lasts so long it becomes practically a family heirloom, so it's worthwhile making the investment.

Serves 2

olive oil
2 sweet potatoes
2 pork loin steaks, about a finger thick
1 tsp honey
1 heaped tbsp English mustard
bunch of spring onions
few drops of Angostura bitters

1. Heat a heavy frying pan with a little olive oil until shimmeringly hot and put the kettle on to boil.

2. Peel the sweet potatoes and slice them thinly. Put them in a pan of boiling water and boil for 7–8 minutes, until cooked through.

3. Dry the pork steaks on kitchen paper and rub with salt and pepper.

4. Put them in the frying pan and cook for 2–3 minutes on each side, until browned and cooked through.

5. Take the pork out and keep on one side.

6. Stir ½ cupful of water, the honey and mustard into the frying pan and let it bubble up. Simmer until nicely thickened.

7. Heat a little olive oil in a small pan. Slice the spring onions diagonally and add to the pan. Cook for 30 seconds, until sizzlingly hot.

8. Drain the potatoes and purée with a hand blender, adding a splash of Angostura bitters.

9. Heap the potatoes onto two plates and top with the pork. Spoon over the sauce and then the spring onions. Eat straight away.

Haricot beans with chorizo and buttered spring greens

Beans on toast for real foodies. This is the sort of supper I could eat five nights out of seven. Do get the best, spiciest chorizo you can, ideally in a chunk rather than sliced, because that's what's flavouring the dish.

Serves 2

1 tbsp olive oil
60g (2oz) chorizo 'picante'
2 x 400g tins of haricot beans
1 clove of garlic, peeled
1 tbsp butter
1 head of spring greens
2 slices of good bread

1. Heat the oil in a medium-sized pan until shimmeringly hot. Slice the chorizo, cutting the slices into halves or quarters. Add to the pan and cook until golden, and the oil has taken on a ruddy hue.

2. Meanwhile, drain and rinse the beans. Crush the garlic into the chorizo pan, stir well, then add the beans. Stir again and pour over enough hot water almost to cover the beans. Simmer for 3–4 minutes, stirring occasionally so that the beans don't catch on the bottom.

3. While the beans cook, sort out the greens. Heat a pan (one with a lid) with the butter and 2 tbsp water until bubbling. Pull away the tough outer leaves of the greens, and rip the tender leaves from their stems. Wash quickly and chop roughly. Add to the hot buttery pan, stir and cover. Cook for 2–3 minutes until wilted, then season generously with salt and pepper.

4. While the greens cook, put the bread in the toaster and get back to the beans. Stir them and draw off the heat. Plunge in a hand blender and blitz briefly, without moving the head, so that just a small portion is puréed. Stir well. The puréed beans should coat the others in a creamy sauce. Add a little more water if necessary, and season with plenty of salt and pepper.

5. Cut the toast in half and put on two plates. Top with the beans. Lift the greens out of the pan (leaving any excess liquid behind) and heap on one side of each plate.

Pork with apple, Calvados sauce and watercress crushed potatoes

I use fairly lean, streaky belly steaks for this, because they have a great flavour, but they are quite chewy. Fillet or loin steaks would be much more tender. You choose. Either way, don't overdo the mustard or it will overwhelm the appley flavour.

Serves 2

3–4 medium potatoes
2 pork steaks, about a finger thick
1 tsp olive oil
1 apple
4 tbsp Calvados
5 tbsp crème fraîche
½ tsp grain mustard (optional)
1 tbsp butter
small bunch of watercress

1. Put the kettle on to boil. Peel and cut the potatoes into dice-sized cubes. Boil in a pan of salted water for about 7 minutes until cooked.

2. Trim most of the fat from the pork and season well with salt and pepper.

3. Meanwhile, heat a heavy frying pan on a medium-high heat. Add the olive oil and then the pork.

4. Cut the apple crossways into pencil-thick slices. Add to the pan with the pork. Turn both after a couple of minutes, when browned. Press down on the pork – this will help it cook through quickly.

5. When the pork is pretty much done, add the Calvados – it will probably catch fire, but don't worry, let the flames die down. Remove the apple and pork to a plate. Add a splash of water to the pan if it looks dry and stir well, scraping up all the gunky brown bits on the bottom of the pan. Stir in the crème fraîche and mustard, if using, taste and season with salt and pepper.

6. Drain the potatoes, add the butter and crush slightly with a spoon or potato masher. Chop the watercress roughly and stir in.

7. Serve the pork and apple with the creamy sauce and the watercress crushed potatoes.

Trim the pork and
boil the spuds

Boil the potatoes in salted water for 7 minutes

Cook the pork over a medium-high heat

Slice the apple crossways and add to the pan

Make the sauce
and crush the
potatoes

Remove the pork and apple – add crème fraîche

Pork with apple, Calvados sauce and watercress crushed potatoes

Trim most of the fat from the pork belly steaks

Season the pork well with salt and pepper

Turn over the pork and apple, and add the Calvados

Cook the pork and apples

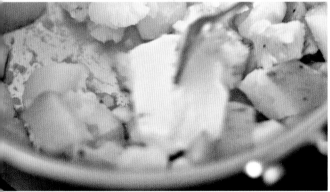

Drain the potatoes, add butter and slightly crush

Add the chopped watercress to the potatoes

'Phast pho'

A pho is a Vietnamese soup made with long-simmered broth, so this is more of a nod to the flavours than an authentic version. Still, it's good and pretty healthy, too.

Serves 2

2 x 300ml tubs of chicken or beef stock
1 clove of garlic, peeled and crushed
thumb of fresh ginger, peeled
pinch of Chinese five spice powder or ground star anise
1 red chilli
1 tbsp Thai fish sauce (nam pla)
bundle (about 60g/2oz) of fine rice noodles
85g (3oz) fillet steak or leftover rare roast beef
1 lime
few sprigs of coriander and mint
handful of beanshoots

1. Tip the stock into a pan and bring to the boil.

2. Add the garlic and use a garlic press to squeeze in 2–3 garlic-clove-sized bits of ginger.

3. Add the five spice powder or star anise. Slice the chilli and add as much as will suit you (taste a sliver to judge the chilli's heat quotient), along with the fish sauce.

4. As soon as the stock boils, add the noodles and cook until just done.

5. Slice the beef very thinly, no thicker than a beermat.

6. Quarter the lime and arrange on a plate with the coriander and mint sprigs and beanshoots.

7. Ladle the soup into two bowls and top with the beef, which will cook in the heat of the stock. Serve with the plate of herbs and beanshoots, and the lime to squeeze over.

5
minutes
to table

Cheese and chorizo quesadillas

It's all too easy to eat too many of these quesadillas, all crisp tortilla and gooily melted cheese, the Mexicans' better answer to the toasted cheese sandwich. Chorizo adds spice, but leave it out for vegetarians and add chopped chilli instead.

Serves 2

dribble of olive oil
2 flour tortillas
lemon-sized hunk of mild, hard cheese (Edam works well)
1 ripe tomato
3 slices of chorizo 'picante'
to serve:
sour cream
small bunch of coriander (optional)

1. Heat the olive oil in a heavy frying pan until shimmeringly hot and put one of the tortillas in. Grate over half the cheese.

2. Slice the tomato and roughly chop the chorizo, and scatter over the cheesy tortilla. Grate the rest of the cheese over this and top with the second tortilla.

3. Peek at the underneath of the quesadilla: if it is looking good and brown, turn it over, otherwise give it a few more seconds. Turning it is the tricky bit. Use a fish slice in one hand and an oven glove on the other, and work fast.

4. Cook on the other side, pressing down with the fish slice to compact the quesadilla.

5. Once brown on both sides, slide it out onto a chopping board and cut into wedges. Serve with a dollop of sour cream and use scissors to snip over a bit of coriander, if you have it.

5
minutes
to table

Chipolatas with red onion gravy, polenta and wilted garlic spinach

For when you want comfort food, and you want it now, here it is: sausages and mash, in double quick time.

Serves 2

1 red onion
1 tbsp olive oil
8–12 chipolata sausages
½ teacupful of quick-cook '1 minute' polenta
1 clove of garlic, peeled and crushed
½ teacupful of red wine
1 tsp honey or redcurrant jelly
1 tbsp butter or a dollop of crème fraîche
for the wilted spinach:
2 tsp butter
2 handfuls of fresh spinach, washed
1 clove of garlic, peeled and crushed

1. Put the kettle on to boil. Heat a large, heavy frying pan until very hot. Peel and slice the onion.

2. Add the oil to the frying pan and start the sausages cooking, turning them in the oil. Add the onion. Stir the mixture from time to time, turning the sausages.

3. Meanwhile, put the polenta in a pan with 2 cupfuls of water and add the crushed garlic. Boil for a couple of minutes, stirring occasionally, until hot and creamy.

4. About 7 minutes after putting the sausages in the pan, splash in the red wine and boil vigorously, stirring all the time. Add the honey or redcurrant jelly and stir well.

5. Melt a knob of butter in a pan. Wash the spinach leaves, if necessary, and add them with a pinch of salt and the crushed garlic. Stir until just starting to wilt.

6. Beat the butter or crème fraîche into the polenta and serve with the sausages, onion gravy and spinach.

Butternut squash, chorizo and prawns

Chorizo is one of those transforming ingredients that adds flavour and colour in spades to any dish. Choose a 'picante' or spicy chorizo for the most punch, and do try to buy sustainably produced prawns.

Serves 2

½ butternut squash
1 red chilli (optional)
olive oil
1 tsp mustard seed (optional)
200g (7oz) or so raw, shelled prawns
60g (2oz) chorizo 'picante'
handful of salad leaves
1 lime

1. Peel the squash with a potato peeler and slice it into pencil-thick rounds (no more, or it won't cook through in time). Thinly slice the chilli, if using. Heat a pan with a splash of olive oil and 1 tsp mustard seed, if using, until shimmeringly hot. Sprinkle the squash with salt and cook in the oil, with the chilli. Turn the squash after 3 minutes or so, until lightly browned.

2. Skewer the prawns on eight bamboo skewers. Heat a little more oil in a heavy frying pan, slice the chorizo and chuck it in. Cook the prawns in the red oil until just done.

3. Mix the squash with a handful of salad leaves (wild rocket is ideal) and pile on a plate. Lay the prawn skewers on top, with the chorizo alongside. Dribble the chorizo oil over and finish with a sqeeze of lime juice.

Huevos revueltos

A Mexican take on scrambled eggs that makes a good supper or brunch dish. Eat them with tortillas or toast.

Serves 2

1 tbsp lard or butter
2 spring onions
2 ripe tomatoes
1 mild red chilli
2 slices of chorizo or salami (optional)
3 eggs
few sprigs of coriander

1. Melt the lard or butter in a heavy frying pan. Chop the spring onions, tomatoes, chilli and chorizo or salami if using, and add to the pan, stirring over a high heat for 1 minute.

2. Beat the eggs lightly with a pinch of salt and add to the pan. Stir until the eggs are set but still creamy.

3. Taste and add salt and pepper, then divide between two plates and scatter with coriander leaves. Eat immediately.

Figs with mozzarella, Parma ham and breadsticks

This isn't exactly a meal in itself, but put it on the table with a board of cheese, some good bread and a bowl of fruit for pudding, and everyone will be happy.

Serves 2

generous handful of wild rocket
3–4 fresh figs
ball of buffalo mozzarella
4 slices of Parma ham
1 tbsp balsamic vinegar
4 tbsp extra-virgin olive oil
1 packet of breadsticks

1. Spread the rocket over a large plate. Cut the figs into eighths and scatter over.

2. Take the buffalo mozzarella and rip it apart with your fingers. Dot the pieces over the rocket and figs.

3. Scrumple up the sheets of Parma ham and nestle them among the other ingredients.

4. Whisk the balsamic vinegar with a fat pinch of salt until the salt has more or less dissolved. Gradually whisk in the olive oil to make a dressing, then trickle over the plate. Serve with the breadsticks.

5
minutes
to table

Lamb kofta skewers with grilled tomatoes and courgettes and homemade hummus

These meatballs on skewers are gorgeous with the hummus, which makes a sort of sauce for the meat and veg. It's traditional to put a spoonful of tahini in hummus, but I've left it out because it isn't strictly necessary and jars of tahini, once bought, can hang around. If you do have some, check that it hasn't gone rancid, which happens quite quickly to tahini that's stored in a cupboard. If it's fine, then by all means add 1 tbsp to the blend, and keep the rest of the jar in the fridge where it will last for ages. Pitta bread is the thing to eat with this.

Serves 2

3 really ripe tomatoes, halved
3 baby courgettes, halved lengthways
for the kofta:
200g (7oz) lamb mince
½ tsp ground cumin
½ tsp ground cinnamon
1 clove of garlic, peeled and crushed
1 egg
for the hummus:
1 x 400g tin of chickpeas, drained and rinsed
1 tsp ground cumin
1 clove of garlic, peeled and crushed
juice of ½ lemon
2 tbsp olive oil
paprika (optional)
to serve:
2 tbsp Greek yoghurt
3–4 sprigs of mint, leaves only
lemon or lime wedges

1. Heat the griddle until very hot. Mix the kofta ingredients together and mould onto 4–6 bamboo skewers. Griddle, turning occasionally, until cooked through.

2. Meanwhile, blitz the hummus ingredients in a food processor with ½ tinful of water until fairly smooth. Taste and add seasoning, plus more water or lemon juice if necessary.

3. Cook the tomatoes and courgettes, cut side down, on the griddle in the lamb juices until just beginning to blacken. Scoop up with a fish slice and arrange on a plate with the kofta.

4. Serve with the hummus (sprinkled with paprika, if you like), Greek yoghurt, mint leaves and lemon or lime wedges.

Get the kofta
cooking first

Mix the kofta ingredients together

Place the hummus ingredients in a food processor

Blitz until well blended and season

Cook the veg
alongside the
kofta

Turn the skewers over when they are brown

Lamb kofta skewers with grilled tomatoes
and courgettes and homemade hummus

Mould the mix onto bamboo skewers

Place the skewers on a hot griddle

Halve the courgettes and tomatoes

Whiz up the hummus

Cook the vegetables in the meat juices

Serve with the hummus and Greek yoghurt

Spring lamb with braised little gems, peas and broad beans and Jersey Royals

I love this combination of spring flavours. Pale spring lamb has a delicate flavour that works well with creamy sauces, but you could use other lamb, too.

Serves 2

1 spring lamb neck fillet
2 tbsp butter, plus a dollop for the potatoes
about 225g (8oz) Jersey Royal new potatoes
2 spring onions
2 little gem lettuces
handful of peas in the pod
handful of broad beans in the pod
3 tbsp crème fraîche
few sprigs of tarragon

1. Put the kettle on to boil. Heat a heavy frying pan until hot. Trim any excess fat or sinew and cut the lamb in half crossways, and then lengthways, to make four thin pieces. Think of the lamb as Toblerone shaped. Sprinkle with salt. Put 1 tbsp butter in the hot pan, then add the lamb and leave to cook, turning every 2 minutes, until browned on all three sides.

2. Meanwhile, half fill a pan with the boiling water and salt it generously. Wash the potatoes and slice thinly. Add them to the boiling water and boil for 7–8 minutes, until cooked.

3. Melt the rest of the butter in a second frying pan (one with a lid). Thinly slice the spring onions and add to the pan. Cut the lettuces in half lengthways and nestle in among the onions. Leave to sizzle while you pod the peas and beans.

4. If the beans are larger than a thumbnail, put them in a sieve and cook them in the pan with the potatoes for 2 minutes, then rinse under a cold tap and slip the grey skins off.

5. Add the peas and beans to the lettuce and stir in the crème fraîche. Put a lid on the pan and cook on a medium-low heat for 3–4 minutes.

6. Take the lamb off the heat and leave to rest for as long as you've got.

7. Roughly chop the tarragon, chucking out any tough stems.

8. Drain the potatoes and stir in a dollop of butter, plus salt and pepper.

9. Divide the braised lettuce and vegetable mixture between two plates. Boil any juices left in the pan to thicken them, add the tarragon and then taste and adjust the seasoning. Slice the lamb and arrange beside the lettuce. Spoon over the sauce. Serve with the potatoes.

A few minutes less: **Leave out the peas and beans, and serve the lamb with just the lettuce and potatoes.**

Thick-cut ham with buttery carrots and a mustardy cream

Carrots cooked in their own juices with butter and herbs, with a slice of good ham, ideally hand cut, but certainly not that strange, wafer-thin formed stuff. What could be nicer, especially with a creamy dollop of mustardy sauce?

Serves 2

3 carrots
1 tbsp butter
few sprigs of herbs – flat-leaf parsley, tarragon, chives, dill, chervil or a mixture
1 tsp grain mustard
2 tbsp thick cream or crème fraîche
2 thick slices of good ham (or 4 thinner slices)

1. Grate the carrots on the coarse side of a box grater.

2. Melt the butter in a frying pan and add the carrots, a pinch of salt and a generous grinding of pepper. Stir until the carrots are hot and wilting.

3. Chop the herbs, throwing out any tough stems, and mix in.

4. Quickly mix together the mustard and cream or crème fraîche.

5. Put the ham on the plates and pile the carrots on top. Dollop the mustardy cream alongside. Eat straight away.

5
**minutes
to table**

Lentils with bacon and balsamic vinegar

Lentils and bacon is one of the great combinations, especially if you can get hold of the slate-green Puy lentils, now available ready cooked in tins and sachets. This is just as good if you use dried lentils and cook them first (follow the instructions on the packet, throwing a couple of peeled cloves of garlic into the cooking water, but not salt, which will toughen the lentils if added before they are properly soft). Of course, the recipe would then take longer than 5 minutes.

Serves 2

3 tbsp olive oil
4 rashers of thin-cut streaky bacon
1 x 400g sachet or tin of cooked Puy lentils
1 clove of garlic, peeled
1 tbsp balsamic vinegar
chilli sauce (optional)
handful of frisée lettuce

1. Heat a heavy frying pan to very hot and add 1 tbsp oil.

2. Snip the bacon across into strips with a pair of scissors and add to the pan. Cook briskly, stir for a minute, until beginning to brown, then add the lentils (drained and rinsed if they came from a tin) and a splash of water (or stock, if you have it).

3. Crush in the clove of garlic and cook, stirring constantly, until really hot.

4. Stir in the balsamic vinegar followed by 2 tbsp olive oil.

5. Taste and season with salt, pepper and maybe a splash of chilli sauce, or a little more oil if the bacon wasn't very fatty. Serve tumbled over the frisée lettuce.

5
minutes
to table

Lamb cutlets with salsa verde, haricot beans and blackened tomatoes

Salsa verde is one of my favourite sauces, an utterly delicious mix of herbs and capers. Here it is almost a salad in its own right. French-trimmed cutlets, with the fat completely removed, cook far more quickly than ordinary lamb chops.

Serves 2

2 tbsp olive oil
4–6 French-trimmed lamb cutlets
2–3 really ripe tomatoes
1 x 400g tin of haricot beans (2 if you are really hungry)
1 clove of garlic, peeled
1 lemon
for the salsa verde:
1 clove of garlic, peeled
4 tinned anchovies in olive oil
small handful of basil
small handful of mint
handful of flat-leaf parsley (you should have twice as much parsley as mint or basil)
1 tbsp capers
1 tbsp coriander seeds
1 tbsp Dijon mustard
olive oil

1. Heat 1 tbsp olive oil in a heavy frying pan until shimmeringly hot. Sprinkle the lamb with salt and cook for about 4 minutes each side until well browned but still pink in the middle. Halve the tomatoes and cook, cut side down, alongside the lamb until nicely charred.

2. Drain the beans and rinse. Heat 1 tbsp oil gently in a saucepan and crush in the garlic. Add the beans and stir well, mashing them a bit against the side of the pan or with a potato masher. Grate in the zest of ½ lemon. Season well with salt and pepper.

3. For the salsa, crush the garlic and anchovies together in a pestle and mortar. Discard any coarse stalks from the herbs and chop them, not too finely. Roughly chop the capers and lightly crush the coriander seeds. Mix the garlic and anchovies with the capers, herbs, coriander seeds and mustard. Stir in enough oil to make a pouring consistency.

4. Taste and add a squeeze of lemon juice if it needs it.

5. Serve the lamb with the beans, tomatoes and lots of salsa verde.

A few minutes less: **Serve the lamb and beans with a dollop of good-quality ready-made pesto (choose one from the chiller cabinet, rather than a jar).**

10 : Birds

minutes
to table

Parmesan chicken, courgettes with tarragon, quinoa and fresh tomato sauce

Quinoa is a Latin American grain, high in protein, that will appeal to anyone who likes couscous. Cooking it in 10 minutes is tight, but just about possible – give it another 2–3 minutes if you prefer it softer.

Serves 2

½ teacupful of quinoa
1 lemon
olive oil
hunk of Parmesan, big enough to grate 4 tbsp
1 tiny clove of garlic, peeled
1 skinless chicken breast fillet
1 egg (or egg white)
3 medium courgettes
1 tbsp butter
3 sprigs of tarragon or a small bunch of dill
3 very ripe tomatoes
1 tsp tomato purée

1. Put the kettle on to boil. Put a saucepan and a heavy frying pan onto the heat. Put the quinoa in the saucepan with a teacupful of boiling water and boil for 9 minutes. Drain if necessary (it should have absorbed pretty much all of the water). Grate over the zest of the lemon, then add a slug of olive oil and season with salt.

2. Meanwhile, grate 4 tbsp Parmesan onto a plate. Crush the garlic and mix in. Cut the chicken breast in half horizontally into two fillets. Put each piece between two pieces of cling film and with a rolling pin bash it out to the thickness of a pound coin. Lightly beat the egg with a pinch of salt. Dip the chicken in the egg and then into the Parmesan, so that it is well coated.

3. Cook the chicken on both sides in the hot frying pan until golden and cooked through.

4. Meanwhile, coarsely grate the courgettes. Melt the butter in another frying pan and add the courgettes. Chop the tarragon or dill (throwing out any tough stalks) and add it to the pan. Fry over a medium-high heat, stirring, until just hot through.

5. Chop the tomatoes finely and mix with a dash of olive oil, a pinch of salt and a grinding of black pepper, plus the tomato purée.

6. Serve the chicken with the quinoa, courgettes and tomato sauce.

A few minutes less: Use couscous instead of quinoa. Put half a teacupful in a bowl, with half a teacupful of boiling water, cover and leave for 5 minutes. Add the lemon zest and seasoning as for the quinoa.

Chicken, pak choi and almond stir-fry

It's worth having a default formula for a stir-fry sauce, and this is mine. By all means vary the vegetables and meat in line with whatever ingredients you have: it'll still be soy-savoury and gratifyingly Oriental in taste.

Serves 2 hungry people

2 sheets of egg noodles
1 tbsp oil
2 cloves of garlic, peeled
handful of blanched almonds
1 skinless chicken breast fillet
1 head of pak choi
4 spring onions
1 medium red chilli (optional)
sesame oil
for the sauce:
1 tbsp soy sauce
1 tbsp grated fresh ginger
2 tbsp dry sherry or Chinese rice wine
1 tsp cornflour
4 tbsp water

1. Put the kettle on to boil. Put the noodles into a pan with a lid, pour over the boiling water, cover and keep to one side.

2. Mix the sauce ingredients together.

3. Heat a wok or large frying pan until hot, then add the oil and heat until almost smoking. Slice the garlic and stir in, cook until golden brown, then scoop it out and throw away.

4. Add the almonds, cook until pale gold, then scoop out and keep to one side.

5. Thinly slice the chicken breast across the grain. Spread the chicken out in the wok, allow to sizzle for a few seconds, then toss until lightly coloured and cooked through, then scoop out.

6. Slice the pak choi. Slice the spring onion diagonally and the chilli into thin rings, if using, and add both to the wok, with a little more oil if necessary. Cook, stirring, for 1 minute, then tip in the pak choi and stir for another minute, until just cooked.

7. Return the cooked chicken and almonds to the wok. Add the sauce and heat through, stirring and tossing everything together, adding a little more water if necessary.

8. Drain the noodles and toss with a few drops of sesame oil. Serve with the stir-fry.

Chicken noodle soup

This was my first '10 minutes to table' recipe and really it could almost be a 5 minute one. I've got more ambitious since then, but I still love this simple broth. Save even more time by using boneless thigh fillets, if you can find them.

Serves 2

2 x 300g tubs of chicken stock
1 capful of whisky (optional)
2 chicken thighs
3 nests of vermicelli
small bunch of dill
small salty crackers, to serve

1. Put the stock in a pan, add the whisky, if using, cover and bring to the boil over a high heat.
2. Meanwhile, strip the skin off the chicken and cut out the bone. Cut the flesh into smallish olive-sized chunks.
3. Once the stock is boiling, add the chicken and the vermicelli. Simmer for 3 minutes or so, until the chicken is cooked through and the vermicelli is cooked.
4. While it simmers, chop the dill, throwing away any tough stalks.
5. Scatter the dill generously over the soup and serve with a few salty crackers.

Noodles with teriyaki sauce and smoked duck

Amazingly popular and very easy. You could use leftover roast duck instead of the smoked duck, or, if you have time, a fresh duck breast – just cook it in a hot frying pan for 5 minutes, skin side down, then turn it and give it 5 minutes on the other side. Let it rest for 10 minutes before slicing it thinly.

Serves 2

2 sheets of fine egg noodles
3 tbsp teriyaki sauce
3 spring onions
1 mild red chilli
1 sliced smoked duck breast
1 tbsp sesame seeds and/or a few sprigs of coriander

1. Put the kettle on to boil. Put the noodles into a pan and cover with the boiling water. Simmer until almost done, leaving a bit of 'bounce' in them. Drain well and mix with the teriyaki sauce.

2. Meanwhile, slice thinly the spring onions, red chilli and smoked duck breast (if it is not already sliced).

3. Toss the noodles with the spring onions, chilli (taste this first to see how hot it is and use only enough to give the noodles a bit of bite) and duck breast.

4. Scatter with the sesame seeds or coriander leaves, or both, and serve.

5
minutes
to table

Chicken with garlic cream cheese sauce

This is a real cheat's recipe, using ready-made garlic and herb cheese. Of course, if you've only got plain cream cheese it'll be as good, better even, with a crushed clove of garlic and chopped herbs stirred in. But this way is easy, and everyone likes it. It is rich though, which is why I've suggested just one chicken breast between two. There's nothing to stop you adding some more vegetables to the sauce to make it more substantial – steamed asparagus or broccoli spring to mind.

Serves 2

1 tbsp butter
1 skinless chicken breast fillet
110g (4oz) garlic and herb cream cheese (such as Boursin)
2 handfuls of washed baby spinach
4 rashers of ready-cooked crispy bacon

1. Heat a heavy frying pan until medium-hot and add the butter.

2. Slice the chicken very thinly across the grain and toss into the pan. Grind over some black pepper and fry the chicken, stirring occasionally, for 2–3 minutes, until cooked through.

3. Add the cream cheese with 3 tbsp water and stir like mad until the chicken is bathed in a hot creamy sauce.

4. Divide the spinach between two bowls and spoon the chicken over. Crumble over the bacon and serve.

5
minutes
to table

Mustard, honey and thyme quail with rosemary potatoes

From the cook's point of view, quail are just miniature chicken, although they do have an extra hint of gamey flavour, particularly on the legs. Flattened out (spatchcocked) and skewered they make a good leisurely meal, with a lot of nibbling of bones.

Serves 2

4 quail (ask the butcher to spatchcock them or follow the instructions below)
1 tsp smooth mustard (Dijon or English, whatever you have)
1 tsp honey
few sprigs of thyme
olive oil
2 handfuls of new potatoes
sprig of rosemary
1 clove of garlic, peeled
bunch of watercress

1. Put the kettle on to boil. Heat the grill to high. Take a heavy roasting tin (one that can go on the hob) and put the quail in, skin side up. Dollop on the mustard and honey, rip over the thyme leaves and rub the mixture all over the skin. Sprinkle with salt and drizzle with olive oil. Grill the quail as close as possible to the heat for 4 minutes, until the skin is well browned, then turn and grill on the other side for 2–3 minutes, until cooked through.

2. Meanwhile, slice the potatoes to the thickness of a pencil, and put in a pan with boiling water from the kettle and a fat pinch of salt. Boil for 5–6 minutes, until almost done then drain.

3. Lift the quail out of the roasting tin onto a serving plate, pull out the skewers and keep warm by the grill.

4. Put the roasting tin on a high heat. Tip in the drained potatoes and rip in the rosemary leaves. Crush in the garlic and stir.

5. Cook the potatoes for 1–2 minutes until beginning to brown. Sprinkle with sea salt and pile onto a plate with the quail. Serve with a bowl of watercress. Eat the quail with your fingers.

To spatchcock quail: With sturdy kitchen scissors, snip down each side of the quail's backbone (throw it away or put it in the stockpot). Pull the quail out to a knock-kneed sunbather position, pushing down hard to flatten the breastbone. Spear a skewer through the tiny drumstick, then the thigh and diagonally across to the wing. Push another skewer across at right angles. Bingo. One spatchcocked quail.

Homemade flatbread, chicken with cardamom and coriander-coconut chutney

I love this creamy chicken, with warm, slightly charred flatbread and fresh green chutney. It's very satisfying to have made the whole lot, too.

Serves 2

bunch of spring onions
1 tbsp olive oil
2 skinless chicken breast fillets
½ tsp ground cardamom or the seeds from 6 pods
2 tbsp flour (any will do)
4 tbsp Greek yoghurt
for the flatbread:
1 heaped teacupful of self-raising flour (150g/5½oz)
1 tbsp olive oil
for the chutney:
3 tbsp desiccated coconut
bunch of fresh coriander
1 clove of garlic, peeled
a few drops of chilli sauce or a green chilli
1 lime
2 tbsp olive oil

1. Put the kettle on to boil. Put the desiccated coconut in a mug and pour over just enough boiling water to cover it. Slice the spring onions. Heat 1 tbsp olive oil in a large, heavy frying pan and stir them in. Cook gently. Cut the chicken into 1cm (⅜ inch) thick slices and stir into the onion pan with the cardamom. Leave to cook while you make the flatbread.

2. Heat a griddle or heavy frying pan to very hot. Mix the flour with a fat pinch of salt, 1 tbsp olive oil and enough water (about 4 tbsp) to make a stiff dough. Divide the dough in two and roll out into rough circles, on a floured surface, to the thickness of a pound coin. Cook on the griddle or pan for about 2 minutes on each side, until slightly charred.

3. Sprinkle 2 tbsp flour into the chicken pan, stir well, and leave until cooked through.

4. Put the coriander leaves in a mini food processor with the garlic, a few drops of chilli sauce (or a piece of green chilli) and the juice of ½ lime. Chop finely or blitz with a hand blender. Drain the coconut (stir the liquid into the chicken pan) and add to the blender along with the olive oil. Blitz briefly to mix it.

5. Stir the yoghurt into the chicken, adding more water, if necessary, to make a creamy sauce.

6. Taste and add salt and pepper. Serve the chicken with the flatbread and coriander chutney.

Soak the coconut
then cook
the chicken

Pour boiling water over the desiccated coconut

Mix the flour with olive oil and water to make a dough

Roll out the dough into two rough circles

Whiz up the
chutney

Drain the coconut: add the liquid to the chicken

Homemade flatbread, chicken with cardamom and coriander-coconut chutney

Slice the spring onions and cook gently

Slice the chicken and add to the pan

Cook on a griddle pan for 2 minutes on each side

Make the flatbread

Blitz the coriander, garlic, chilli, lime and coconut

Add the yoghurt to the chicken and stir

Chicken and chive Caesar salad with homemade garlic croûtons

A proper Caesar salad is made with a dressing like this, which includes a part-cooked egg. Adding chicken has become a modern tradition, and it does turn the salad into a good meal. If you prefer, leave the chicken out and scatter over some tinned or bottled anchovy fillets, the dark pinkish-brown kind, not the pale silvery sort, which are too vinegary.

Serves 2

1 skinless chicken breast fillet
olive oil
1 plain bagel or bread roll
1 clove of garlic, peeled
1 head of romaine lettuce
small bunch of chives
for the dressing:
1 egg
hunk of Parmesan, enough to grate 3 tbsp, plus extra for topping
1 small clove of garlic, peeled
6 tbsp olive oil
1 tsp Dijon mustard
2 tsp Worcestershire sauce
juice of ½ lemon

1. Put the kettle on to boil. Heat a griddle or heavy frying pan until very hot. Cut the chicken in half horizontally to make two thin escalopes. Beat them with your fist or a mallet to make them thinner still (around twice the thickness of a one pound coin). Rub them with olive oil, sprinkle with salt and cook them on the griddle or pan on both sides until cooked through.

2. For the dressing, cook the egg in boiling water for 1 minute, then drain and cool in cold water.

3. Meanwhile, cut the clove of garlic in half. Thinly slice the bagel or bread roll, rub with the cut clove of garlic and drizzle with olive oil. Toast on the griddle until crisp.

4. Wash the lettuce leaves, dry and wrap in a tea towel. Chill in the fridge. Chop the chives.

5. Grate 3 tbsp Parmesan, crack in the egg and whiz together with the rest of the dressing ingredients using a hand blender or a mini food processor.

6. Pull the leaves of the romaine lettuce apart and put on two plates. Chuck the chicken on the leaves and pour over the dressing. Sprinkle with chives and grate over more Parmesan if you like and scatter over the croûtons.

Salad of rotisserie chicken

This is the sort of salad I might throw together for lunch after a summer holiday trip to a French market, with still warm chicken and olives from the olive stand. If I can get potatoes cooked in the chicken fat too, so much the better. The salad works just as well back home, especially if you can find free-range rotisserie chickens. This is really a salad for four, but two hungry people could probably do it justice. If there is some left over, it keeps well until supper, the fennel softening nicely in the dressing.

Serves 2

1 small roasted chicken
1 bulb of fennel
handful of green olives (the kind with chilli and lemon are best)
1 small clove of garlic, peeled
1 lemon
olive oil

1. Rip the chicken off the bone in large chunks.

2. Slice the fennel as thinly as you can and put in a large bowl with the chicken and olives.

3. Tip the juices from the chicken bag into a bowl, crush in the garlic and grate in all the zest from the lemon. Squeeze in the juice from half the lemon, taste and add enough olive oil to make a pleasingly lemony dressing.

4. Dribble the dressing over the salad and mix well.

5
minutes
to table

Cold chicken, dill, mint and rocket salad

White food is somehow soothing, perhaps because its milkiness reminds us of childhood. This creamy salad, bright with green herbs, is particularly restorative and calming made with the leftover turkey after Christmas.

Serves 2

a few sprigs of mint
a few sprigs of dill
3 tbsp crème fraîche
teacupful of cold chicken or turkey meat
handful of wild rocket or watercress
2 tbsp toasted pine nuts (optional)

1. Chop the mint and dill, throwing out any tough stalks (you're looking for about 2 tbsp chopped herbs in total), and mix with the crème fraîche. Rip the cold chicken or turkey meat into pieces and stir in.

2. Add 1–2 tbsp water so that the mixture has a soft, creamy consistency. Taste and season with salt and pepper.

3. Gently mix the chicken with the rocket or watercress. Sprinkle on the pine nuts, if you like, and eat straight away.

5
minutes
to table

Warm salad of baby spinach, chicken livers and bacon

A bistro classic, this one, easy and cheap to throw together at home. Eat it with a glass of gutsy red wine.

Serves 2

4 rashers of streaky bacon
6 tbsp olive oil
200g (7oz) chicken livers
1 slice of day-old bread
2 handfuls of baby spinach
2 tbsp balsamic vinegar

1. Cut the bacon into strips. Heat a frying pan with 2 tbsp olive oil, add the bacon and cook until golden. Take out and keep on one side.

2. Meanwhile, cut the chicken livers into mouthful-sized pieces, getting rid of any greenish bits, which will taste bitter.

3. Cut the bread into cubes, throwing away the crusts. Add 1 tbsp olive oil to the bacon pan and fry the bread cubes until golden.

4. Scoop them out. Fry the chicken livers until browned on the outside and pink inside.

5. Divide the spinach between two bowls and top with the livers, bacon and croûtons.

6. Add 2 tbsp water and the balsamic vinegar to the pan and stir vigorously, scraping up the gunky bits. Add the rest of the oil, then taste and season with salt and pepper.

7. Pour the dressing over the salad. Eat immediately.

Green chicken curry

This is a nod to a Thai curry, although aficionados will be quick to notice that it is not authentic – no shrimp paste, no holy basil, no lots of things. Never mind – it hits the right buttons when you want a whiff of south-east Asia, on a tight budget and without a cupboard full of esoteric ingredients. Oh yes, and in 10 minutes. Boiled rice is the thing to eat with this, but it's impossible to cook rice from scratch in less that 12 minutes, so use a pouch of cooked rice for the microwave. Even without a microwave, the rice can be spread out in a steamer and reheated over a pan of boiling water in 3–4 minutes.

Serves 2

2 chicken thighs
3 courgettes or other veg
bunch of spring onions
1 green chilli or a splash of chilli sauce
1 tsp fresh ginger, peeled
1 clove of garlic, peeled
1 tbsp vegetable oil
1 tsp turmeric
50g (1¼oz) coconut cream
bunch of coriander, stems only (save the leaves for another dish)
1 tbsp Thai fish sauce (nam pla)

1. Put the kettle on to boil. Pull the skin from the chicken thighs and cut away the bone. Cut the flesh into large chunks. Cut the courgettes into quarters lengthways and slice each into short pieces. Keep six pieces to one side for the sauce. Slice the spring onions thinly. Chop the green chilli, if using. Grate the ginger and garlic.

2. Heat the oil in a large pan, add the chicken and cook over a high heat for 2 minutes, stirring often, until it is light golden in colour. Add the spring onions and cook for 1 minute, then stir in the courgettes, chilli, ginger, garlic and turmeric.

3. Put the coconut cream into a jug and pour over a small mugful (about 110ml/4fl oz) of boiling water. Stir until the cream has dissolved. Chop the stems of the coriander and add to the jug with the six pieces of courgette. Blitz to a purée with a hand blender.

4. Pour the cream mixture into the pan and simmer briefly. Check the chicken is cooked through. Stir in the fish sauce, taste and check the seasoning. Serve with boiled white rice.

A few minutes less: Buy a good-quality, green curry paste, adding it at the same time as the courgettes, and instead of the chilli, ginger, garlic and turmeric. But try to use fresh coriander, nothing else tastes the same.

Crisp chicken with herb yoghurt dip and a winter salad

This is nothing more than posh chicken nuggets, and a tremendous crowd pleaser. The salad of winter vegetables is a good way to avoid buying yet another bag of imported leaves.

Serves 2

vegetable oil, for frying
2 skinless chicken breast fillets
2 slices of day-old bread
1 clove of garlic, peeled
hunk of Parmesan, enough to grate 2 tbsp (optional)
1 egg
3 tbsp plain flour (any will do)
for the winter salad:
2 Jerusalem artichokes
1 blood orange
1 head of chicory
olive oil
squeeze of lemon juice
1 punnet of cress
for the yoghurt dip:
1 lemon (zest and a squeeze of juice)
6 tbsp Greek yoghurt
bunch of coriander

1. Heat the oil about 0.5cm (¼ inch) deep in a heavy frying pan until shimmeringly hot. Slice the chicken into strips 1cm (⅜ inch) thick.

2. Cut the crusts from the bread and whiz in a mini food processor with the garlic and a pinch of salt. Grate in 2 tbsp Parmesan if you like, and mix well. Beat the egg with a pinch of salt.

3. Dip the chicken pieces in the flour, then the egg, then the breadcrumbs, making sure each strip is well coated. Fry in the oil until golden and cooked through. Drain on kitchen paper.

4. Peel and slice the artichokes thinly and place in a bowl of water. Peel and slice the orange with a sharp knife, or just skin the segments. Break the chicory head into individual leaves.

5. Drain the artichoke and toss together with the chicory leaves and orange segments. Add about 1 tbsp oil. Taste the mix and add a squeeze of lemon juice if it needs it. Mix in most of the cress and tumble onto a plate. Snip over the rest of the cress.

6. Grate the zest from the lemon. Blend the yoghurt, coriander leaves and zest together into a smoothish dip. Taste and add a squeeze of lemon juice if necessary.

Slice the chicken and make the breadcrumbs

Slice the chicken into 1cm (⅜ inch) strips

Dip the chicken in the flour first

Then dip the chicken in the beaten egg

Fry the chicken then make the salad and dip

Fry the chicken in hot oil until crisp and golden

Crisp chicken with herb yoghurt dip and a winter salad

Put the bread and garlic in a mini food processor

Whiz to make breadcrumbs

Finally coat the chicken in the breadcrumbs

Coat the chicken in breadcrumbs

Slice the orange. Mix with the chicory and artichokes

Blend the yoghurt, coriander and lemon zest

Duck breast with soft polenta and caramelized carrots

A large duck breast per person is a pretty big helping, and most people will be happy with one between two. Cook it simply with semi-caramelized carrots and creamy soft polenta and, perhaps, a posy of watercress on the plate too.

Serves 2

1 or 2 duck breasts
4 medium carrots
2 tbsp butter
1 tsp honey
½ teacupful of quick-cook '1 minute' polenta
1 clove of garlic, peeled
small bunch of flat-leaf parsley

1. Put the kettle on to boil. Heat a heavy frying pan until hot. Dry the duck breast skin with kitchen paper and rub with salt. Cut in half lengthways. Put skin side down in the pan and leave to sizzle. Turn every 2–3 minutes and, when cooked on all sides (it will still be pink in the middle), put it on a plate to rest.

2. Meanwhile, slice the carrots and put them in a pan with a lid with 1 tbsp butter, the honey, a pinch of salt and about 2 tbsp water. Cover and cook over a medium heat, shaking and stirring the pan frequently.

3. Put the polenta in a pan with 2 teacupfuls of water. Crush in the garlic, stir and leave to simmer. Once it is cooked chop the parsley and stir it into the polenta, along with 1 tbsp butter. Taste and add salt and pepper.

4. Slice the duck. Dollop the polenta on two plates and serve with the duck and carrots.

Smoked chicken with pecan nuts and sherry vinegar on radicchio

This winter salad is a good one to make ahead, because unlike most salad leaves, radicchio doesn't mind waiting around. Use ordinary cooked chicken instead of the smoked chicken if you like, and balsamic or wine vinegar instead of the sherry vinegar.

Serves 2

4 tsp honey
2 tbsp shelled pecan nuts
1 smoked chicken portion
1 tbsp sherry vinegar
4 tbsp olive oil
1 radicchio

1. Heat 2 tsp honey, a pinch of salt and a good grinding of black pepper in a small pan. Add the pecan nuts and turn until coated, then raise the heat and allow them to colour a bit. Tip out onto a plate to cool.

2. Rip the chicken into small pieces.

3. Whisk the vinegar with a pinch of salt and the remaining 2 tsp honey, then gradually whisk in the oil.

4. Tear the radicchio apart into leaves and toss in half the dressing. Top with the chicken and pecans, then drizzle over the last of the dressing.

5
minutes
to table

Club sandwich with lettuce, avocado, crisp bacon and turkey

Of course cold chicken would do just as well as turkey here, but somehow this combination shouts Boxing Day to me.

Serves 2

6 slices of good bread
1 teacupful of roast turkey or roast chicken meat
a few chives
2 tbsp crème fraîche or mayonnaise
4 large lettuce leaves
1 ripe avocado
4 rashers of ready-cooked crisp bacon

1. Toast the bread. Chop the poultry meat and the chives quickly and mix with 1 tbsp crème fraîche or mayonnaise. Divide between two pieces of toast and top with the lettuce.

2. Cut the avocado in half, scoop out the stone and with a table knife score the flesh deeply in a crisscross pattern, going down to, but not through, the skin. Scoop the flesh out with a dessertspoon.

3. Season the avocado with salt and pepper and mix with the rest of the crème fraîche or mayonnaise. Crumble in the bacon and stir. Taste and add extra seasoning if necessary.

4. Divide the mixture between two more slices of toast. Stack them on top of the lettuce and turkey (or chicken) and top with a final two slices of toast. Cut each sandwich in half diagonally and serve.

5
minutes
to table

Thai turkey nam jim

This zingy salad is a great way to use up the remains of a cold turkey or any cold meat. Nam jim is a classsic Thai dressing and this recipe is based on one given to me by the chef Paul Gayler. It should be a good balance of hot, sour, sweet and salty.

Serves 2

1 iceberg lettuce
1 carrot
a few leaves of Chinese leaf lettuce, beansprouts, or cucumber
2 teacupfuls of cold cooked turkey or chicken meat
a few peanuts (optional)
bunch of watercress
6 sprigs of mint
1 red chilli (optional)
for the dressing:
½ green chilli
1 tiny shallot
½ clove of garlic, peeled
bunch of coriander leaves, plus the washed roots if still attached to the bunch
1½ tsp brown sugar
1½ tsp Thai fish sauce (nam pla)
juice of 1–2 limes

1. Carefully prise the outer leaves off the iceberg lettuce to make lettuce bowls. Shave the carrot into thin ribbons with a potato peeler. Cut the Chinese leaf crossways into narrow strips or the cucumber into sticks, if using. Cut the turkey or chicken into slivers. Heat a frying pan and toast the peanuts, if using, until they are patched with dark brown.

2. Pull the seeds out of the green chilli and chop it, then peel and chop the shallot too. Whiz together the garlic, shallot and ½ tsp sea salt in a mini food processor. Add the coriander roots, if you have them, and whiz again.

3. Add the coriander leaves (save a few for the garnish), chilli, sugar, nam pla and lime juice, and whiz again. Taste and check there is a good balance of hot, salty, sweet and sour.

4. Mix the turkey or chicken, carrot and Chinese leaf (or beansprouts or cucumber).Chop off any tough ends of the watercress stalks. Stir the watercress and the mint leaves into the salad with the dressing. Pile into the iceberg bowls and scatter with the peanuts and coriander leaves, and a little sliced red chilli if you like.

A few minutes less: Make a spicy dressing by mixing 1 tbsp ready-made harissa with 3 tbsp olive oil and 2 tsp lemon juice. Season with salt and pepper and use to dress the salad. Serve with a good dollop of plain yoghurt.

10 : Fish
minutes to table

Salmon, purple-sprouting broccoli, anchovy butter and new potatoes

If you think you hate anchovies, try this: a savoury, simple butter sauce, without fishiness, that's gorgeous with broccoli and salmon. Purple-sprouting broccoli used to be an early spring treat, but now it's available from October. Ordinary broccoli (which we ought to call calabrese, but never do) works well too, as do French beans.

Serves 2

280g (10oz) new potatoes (Jersey Royals are good)
6 stems of purple-sprouting broccoli
2 pieces of organically farmed salmon fillet
4 tbsp butter, plus 1 tsp for the potatoes
3 anchovies in olive oil
scrap of garlic, peeled
½ bunch of chives

1. Put the kettle on to boil, and use some of the water to half fill a smallish pan. Slice the potatoes 0.5cm (¼ inch) thick, chucking out the ends. Add to the pan with a good pinch of salt and boil for 6–8 minutes, until cooked through. Drain.

2. Meanwhile, trim the tough ends off the broccoli and use the rest of the boiling water to cook the florets for 3–4 minutes until just tender. Drain.

3. Heat a heavy frying pan until hot. Pat the salmon dry with kitchen paper and rub the skin with salt. Heat 1 tsp butter in the pan and add the salmon skin side down. Cook for 3 minutes, until the skin is golden, then turn and cook on the other side for another 2 minutes, or until cooked through.

4. Meanwhile, pound the anchovies and garlic in a pestle and mortar. Add the rest of the butter and pound again to a chunky paste.

5. Mix the broccoli with a dollop of the anchovy butter and arrange on two plates with the fish. Dollop the rest of the anchovy butter on top of the fish. Chop the chives and stir with 1 tsp butter into the drained potatoes, and add to the plates. Serve immediately.

Vermicelli con vongole

Pasta with clams, simple but glamorous.... Put a big empty bowl on the table for the clam shells.

Serves 2

4–6 nests of vermicelli, depending on your hunger
450g (1lb) tiny clams
2 tbsp olive oil
2 cloves of garlic, peeled
½ glass of white wine (about 5 tbsp)
1 ripe tomato
1 mild red chilli
small bunch of flat-leaf parsley
1 tsp lemon zest

1. Put a saucepan on the heat and put the kettle on to boil. Fill the hot saucepan with boiling water (heating the pan first helps the water come back to the boil quickly) and, when bubbling again drop in the vermicelli. Cook for the time recommended on the packet (usually 2–3 minutes).

2. Meanwhile, rinse the clams well with cold water and scrub. Chuck out any that don't close when you tap the shell against the sink, and any with broken shells.

3. Meanwhile, heat 2 tbsp oil in a pan and crush in the garlic. Stir, then pour in the wine and add the clams. Cover and cook over a high heat while you chop the tomato and chilli, then add them to the pan too, shaking well. Cook until all the clam shells are open, about 1 minute.

4. Chop the parsley. Drain the pasta, reserving a teacupful of water, and return the pasta to the pan. Scoop the clams and tomatoes into the pasta pan with the parsley and grate in the lemon zest.

5. Pour in the juice from the clams, leaving behind any grit that's collected in the bottom of the pan. Toss everything together, adding some of the saved pasta water, if necessary, to make a nice consistency, and grind in some black pepper. Pile into two bowls (throw away any clams that haven't opened) and serve with napkins.

5
minutes
to table

Sauce vierge with scallops

Try to find hand-dived scallops in the shell for this and ask the fishmonger to prepare them for you. Loose scallops are often dredged, which does long-term damage to the sea bed. Hand-dived scallops are expensive, so this is a treat, but worth it for an occasional blow out. All you need is some good bread to go with it.

Serves 2

1 tsp butter
5 tbsp extra-virgin olive oil, plus 1 tsp, for frying
6–10 scallops with their roe, depending on the size
1 shallot
2 really ripe tomatoes (plum ones are best)
2 sprigs of basil
1 small clove of garlic, peeled
squeeze of lemon juice

1. Heat a large frying pan with the butter and 1 tsp oil until shimmeringly hot.

2. Pat the scallops dry on kitchen paper and prick the roes with the point of a knife to stop them bursting. Add to the pan and cook for 1 minute on each side, until just coloured.

3. Meanwhile, peel and chop the shallot (use a mini food processor if that's quicker for you, but don't blend it to a purée). Chop the tomatoes into pea-sized pieces and shred the basil, saving the little leaves at the top for the garnish.

4. Put the tomatoes, shallot and basil in a small pan with the extra-virgin olive oil. Crush in the garlic and warm gently. Taste and season with salt and pepper. Squeeze in a little lemon juice if necessary.

5. Scoop the scallops onto plates and add the sauce to the scallop pan. Stir vigorously and quickly pour over and around the scallops. Add the little basil leaves and serve.

5
minutes
to table

Fresh sardines with parsley, spring onions and Jersey Royals

You might be able to persuade your fishmonger to bone your sardines, but many are reluctant so I've included instructions for this too, just in case. The truth is, you'll never get rid of every bone in this notoriously bony fish, but the little ones left behind shouldn't give too much trouble. Cook the sardines simply with this bright-flavoured, sherry vinegar-sharp dressing to spoon over.

Serves 2

140g (5oz) Jersey Royals or other new potatoes
4–6 sardines, gutted and heads removed
2 tbsp flour
olive oil
4 spring onions
small bunch of flat-leaf parsley
1 tbsp sherry vinegar

1. Put the kettle on to boil. Wash the potatoes and cut into small chunks. Put them in a pan, cover with boiling water and boil for about 8 minutes, until cooked.

2. Meanwhile, open out the belly of a sardine and lay it splayed open, skin side up, on a board. Press down firmly along the backbone to loosen it. Turn the fish over and with kitchen scissors, snip the end of the backbone at the tail end and remove it. Use a sharp knife to get rid of any obvious bones which are left. Repeat with the rest of the sardines.

3. Mix the flour with a pinch of salt and some pepper and use this mixture to coat the sardines. Heat 1 tbsp oil in a heavy frying pan until shimmeringly hot and fry the sardines for 1 minute or so on each side until cooked through.

4. Chop the spring onions and parsley leaves into peppercorn-sized pieces. Mix with the vinegar and 3 tbsp oil.

5. Drain the potatoes and trickle with a little olive oil and sprinkle with sea salt. Grind over plenty of black pepper.

6. Give each person 2–3 sardines, some potatoes and a generous helping of the parsley and spring onion dressing.

Get the potatoes
cooking first

Wash the potatoes and cut into small chunks

Mix the flour with a pinch of salt and some pepper

Coat the sardines in the seasoned flour

Chop up the
dressing

Chop the spring onions and parsley

Fresh sardines with parsley, spring onions and Jersey Royals

Boil the potatoes for about 8 minutes

Open out each sardine's belly and remove bones

Heat the oil in a frying pan and add the sardines

Fry the sardines

Mix with the vinegar and olive oil

Turn the sardines over and cook until done

Crisp fish with minted mushy peas

Gorgeous, grown-up fish fingers, which children love too. The minted peas have enough starch for you to forgo potatoes but, with not too much practice, you could slice a few and cook them in boiling water and still be under 10 minutes.

Serves 2

1 tbsp butter
375g (13oz) frozen peas
about 400g (14oz) white fish fillet, skinless and boneless – pollock or Marine
  Stewardship Council (MSC) certified sustainable cod
2 tbsp plain flour (any will do)
1 egg
4 tbsp breadcrumbs
olive oil spray
sprig of mint
2 lemon quarters

1. Put the kettle on to boil. Heat the grill to high. Put a pan on the stove and add the butter and ½ teacupful of boiling water. Add the peas, cover and give a good shake. Cook over a medium-high heat while you prepare the fish.

2. Cut the fish into long fat fingers. Mix the flour with a good pinch of salt and plenty of pepper, and toss the fish in it. Beat the egg lightly with 1 tbsp water. Toss the fish pieces into the egg, then, one by one, dip into the breadcrumbs, turning each piece so that it is well coated. Place on the grill tray, spray with oil and grill for 2 minutes, until golden. Turn, spray again and grill for 2 minutes more, until cooked through.

3. While the fish is cooking, chop the mint leaves. Give the peas a good stir and check they are hot through. Remove the lid to boil off most of the liquid. With a hand blender, blitz to a rough purée, taste and season with salt and pepper. Stir in the mint.

4. Serve the fish with a good dollop of pea purée and the lemon quarters.

Fillet of plaice with beurre noisette and capers

Beurre noisette, just butter cooked until it goes brown and nutty smelling, is one of the great sauces for fish, and it takes almost no time to prepare.

Serves 2

3 tbsp butter (salted is best)
2 slender fillets of plaice (other white fish will work too)
3–4 sprigs of flat-leaf parsley or chervil
2 tbsp capers in vinegar
½ lemon
2 chunks of good bread, or boiled potatoes if time allows

1. Heat 1 tsp butter in a heavy frying pan over a high heat, add the plaice and cook for 2–3 minutes, until just barely cooked through.

2. Chop the parsley or chervil.

3. Slide the fish onto plates, add the rest of the butter to the pan and cook until it turns brown.

4. Add the capers and parsley or chervil, plus a squeeze of lemon juice, taste to check the seasoning and pour over the fish. Eat with a chunk of good bread, or if you have a few extra minutes some boiled potatoes.

5
minutes
to table

Seared tuna with beans and artichokes

It's worth shelling out for good-quality artichokes for this, because the cheap ones can be tasteless. If you come across them, snap up frozen artichoke hearts (try Marks & Spencer) or frozen artichoke bottoms, often found in ethnic shops. Chop roughly and quickly defrost them by heating through in a frying pan with a little olive oil.

Serves 2

2 tuna steaks
olive oil
1 x 400g tin of cannellini beans
1 small red onion
1 jar of artichoke hearts or 1 teacupful of frozen
a few black olives
1 tbsp red wine vinegar
1 tsp Dijon mustard
3 sprigs of flat-leaf parsley or chervil

1. Heat a griddle or heavy frying pan until very hot. Rub the tuna with olive oil, sprinkle with salt and cook the steaks for about 1 minute on each side until cooked but still slightly pink in the middle.

2. Meanwhile, drain and rinse the beans. Peel and finely slice the red onion and mix with the beans, artichoke hearts and olives.

3. Mix 3 tbsp olive oil with the vinegar and mustard, season with salt and pepper and stir into the bean mixture.

4. Chop the parsley or chervil and add that too. Pile onto two plates and top with the tuna.

5
minutes
to table

English salade niçoise with basil dressing

Loyd Grossman, my co-presenter on the '10 minutes to table' videos castigated me for using fresh tuna in a niçoise-type salad. Maybe he's right and tinned is more authentic. I still like fresh best, especially in this summery salad that uses English ingredients in a French classic.

Serves 2

handful of new potatoes
2 hen or pheasant eggs or 4 quail eggs
4 runner beans (no more than 20cm/8in long)
7 or so peapods
4–6 small ripe tomatoes
2 small tuna steaks (look for line-caught yellowfin)
handful of wild rocket, pea shoots or little gem lettuce leaves
1 small mild onion or spring onion, thinly sliced
a few olives
for the basil dressing:
small bunch of basil
1 tsp Dijon mustard
1 tsp wine vinegar (red wine vinegar is best)
4 tbsp olive oil
1 anchovy in olive oil

1. Put the kettle on to boil. Heat a heavy frying pan or griddle until very hot. Slice the potatoes thinly and put to boil in a pan of boiling water for 7 minutes. Add the eggs and boil until they are done to your liking – either soft or hard boiled. Scoop them out and peel them.

2. Meanwhile, trim the beans and slice thinly on the diagonal. Cook in another pan of salted boiling water for 2–3 minutes. Pod the peas and add for the last minute or so. Drain and run under a cold tap until completely cold. While the beans are boiling, drop the tomatoes in the water for 10 seconds. Scoop out, slip off the skins and cut the tomatoes into quarters.

3. To make the dressing, pop the basil into a small sieve and lower into one of the pans of boiling water for 5 seconds or so, until it wilts. Lift out and run under cold water to cool. Squeeze dry in a tea towel. In a mini food processor blend the basil with the mustard, vinegar, oil and anchovy. Taste and check the seasoning.

4. Season the tuna steaks with salt, rub with a little olive oil and cook in the hot frying pan for 1 minute or so on each side until cooked but still slightly pink in the middle. Slice into three.

5. Scatter the rocket, pea shoots or lettuce leaves on a large plate. Toss in a little of the dressing. Drain the potatoes and mix with a little dressing, and arrange on the lettuce. Add the beans, peas, tomatoes, tuna, onion, olives and eggs. Dribble over the dressing.

Pan-fried rainbow trout with pine nuts, lemon and garlic spinach and pink fir apple potatoes

Rainbow trout is not the most thrilling of fish, but it is inexpensive and easy to get hold of, so it makes sense to learn to love it, or at least like it. This is a good way to do that, an updated version of that hotel classic, trout with almonds. The toasty pine nuts are perfect with the sweet, soft flesh.

Serves 2

about 200g (8oz) pink fir apple potatoes
4 tbsp butter
1 tbsp flour
4 rainbow trout fillets
1 lemon
1 clove of garlic, peeled
4 handfuls of fresh spinach
60g (2oz) pine nuts
sprig of oregano or marjoram

1. Put the kettle on to boil. Slice the potatoes as thick as a pound coin and cook in a pan of salted boiling water for 8 minutes, until just done. Drain and toss with 1 tbsp of butter.

2. Meanwhile, melt 1 tbsp butter in a heavy frying pan. Put the flour onto a plate and mix in a pinch of salt and a grinding of black pepper. Dip both sides of the fish fillets in the mixture, then fry for 2 minutes on each side until golden and cooked through.

3. Cut the lemon in half and cut one half into wedges. Melt 1 tbsp butter in a saucepan, grate in the zest of the other lemon half and crush in the garlic. Stir in the spinach. Let it wilt in the heat.

4. Lift out the cooked fish onto two plates and wipe out the pan with kitchen paper. Heat the last 1 tbsp of butter and add the pine nuts. Sizzle until the pine nuts are golden and add a few leaves of oregano or marjoram. Pour over the fish.

5. Lift the spinach out of the pan leaving any excess juice behind, and pile onto the plates. Pour some of the spinach juices on the potatoes, and serve with the fish, spinach and lemon wedges.

Tom yam soup

This fast soup is sinus-clearingly hot and sour, perfect to shake off a cold or just the winter blues. It's delicious cold in the summer, too.

Serves 2

2 x 300ml tubs of chicken stock
2 limes
1 hot red chilli
1 spring onion
2 tbsp Thai fish sauce (nam pla)
some fat, raw peeled prawns or slivers of cooked chicken
4 sprigs of coriander

1. Bring the stock to the boil and squeeze in the juice of both limes.

2. Slice the chilli and spring onion and add them to the stock, along with the fish sauce. Stir in the prawns, if using, and as soon as they are opaque, take the pan off the heat.

3. This is the point to add the chicken, if that's your protein of choice. Either way, rip in the whole coriander leaves and serve.

5
minutes
to table

Crab cakes

If you can get hold of some fresh, white crab meat this is a great way to eat it. Frozen crab meat is pretty good too and even tinned, although it doesn't taste of very much, has a certain charm, and will work here as long as you use plenty of seasoning.

Serves 2

1 thick slice of day-old bread
small bunch of flat-leaf parsley
1 egg
½ tsp Worcestershire sauce
3 tbsp crème fraîche
225g (8oz) cooked white crab meat, flaked
butter and oil, for frying
handful of watercress

1. Heat a heavy frying pan until medium hot. Blitz the bread to crumbs in a mini food processor. Add the parsley leaves and whiz again until the crumbs are flecked with green.

2. Beat the egg and mix with the Worcestershire sauce and 1 tbsp crème fraîche. Add the crab meat and about 4 tbsp of the breadcrumbs. (Tip the rest of the crumbs into a saucer.) Season with salt and pepper and combine well, but gently, so you don't break up the crab meat flakes.

3. Divide the mixture into four portions and flatten gently into thick patties. Coat each patty lightly with the remaining crumbs.

4. Melt enough butter and a little oil to cover generously the bottom of a frying pan, and heat until medium hot. Add the crab patties, in batches if necessary, and fry for about 1–2 minutes each side, until golden brown and hot through.

5. Remove from pan and drain on kitchen paper. Serve straight away with the rest of the crème fraîche and watercress.

A few minutes more: Refrigerate the patties for 20–30 minutes before frying to make them easier to handle.

5
minutes
to table

Harissa mackerel with fennel, black olive salad and mint couscous

Spicy grilled fish with a quick herb couscous and a Moroccan-inspired salad. Harissa, the north African paste, is a great store cupboard staple, but use it with caution, because it can be very hot indeed. I like the Belazu rose harissa, which is expensive but well balanced.

Serves 2

1 tsp harissa
tomato purée (optional)
olive oil
1 lime
2 small mackerel, gutted and heads removed, or one large one, filleted
½ teacupful of couscous
1 head of fennel
handful of black olives
1 spring onion
a few sprigs of mint and flat-leaf parsley
plain yoghurt, to serve

1. Put the kettle on to boil. Heat a heavy frying pan (or a barbecue) until very hot. Taste the harissa and if it is impossibly hot mix it with equal parts of tomato purée and olive oil until it tastes acceptable.

2. Halve the lime. Cut 4 thin slices of lime and quarter them. Slash the skin of the mackerel several times and push in the lime slices. Smear the harissa over both sides of the mackerel and cook in the hot pan for 4 minutes, then turn and cook for 4 minutes on the other side, or until cooked through.

3. Put the couscous in a bowl and pour over ½ teacupful of boiling water. Add a pinch of salt and a splash of olive oil. Cover and put to one side.

4. Slice the fennel thinly. Pit the olives. Mix together and season with salt. Grate over some lime zest, using the bigger piece of lime, and squeeze on a little lime juice.

5. Slice the spring onion, chop the herbs (throwing away any tough stalks) and mix into the couscous. Taste and check the seasoning. You could add some lime zest and juice to the couscous too, if you like.

6. Cut the spare ½ lime into lime wedges. Serve with the mackerel, fennel salad, couscous and a bowl of plain yoghurt.

Salt and pepper squid with cucumber salad and Asian dipping sauce

This is a classic, a sort of Oriental take on onion rings. Do make sure that the oil is hot enough or the rings will be soggy not crisp. It should spit and splutter if you flick a drop of water in.

Serves 2

vegetable oil for frying
½ tsp mixed peppercorns
5 tbsp cornflour
½ tsp sea salt
300g (11oz) cleaned squid
for the cucumber salad:
½ cucumber
4 spring onions
a few sprigs of mint, basil and coriander
for the dipping sauce:
2 tbsp fish sauce
1 lime
1 tsp sugar (any kind will do)
red chilli (optional)

1. Fill a deep pan no more than a third full of oil and put it on a high heat.

2. Smash the peppercorns roughly in a pestle and mortar and mix with the cornflour and salt. Slice the squid 0.5cm (¼ inch) thick and trim off the hard top bit of the tentacles. Dredge the pieces in the cornflour mixture.

3. Halve the cucumber lengthways and scrape out the seeds with a teaspoon. Shave it in ribbons with a vegetable peeler. Slice the spring onions.

4. To make a dipping sauce, mix the fish sauce, 1 tbsp lime juice, the sugar and a little finely chopped chilli, if you like.

5. Rip the mint, basil and coriander leaves, throwing away any tough stalks. Toss the cucumber, onions and ripped herbs together with 1 tbsp dipping sauce.

6. When the oil is shimmeringly hot drop in all the squid and cook for 1 minute or so until browned and crisp. (I didn't let the oil get hot enough and mine, shown in this photo, didn't brown properly!) Scoop out with a slotted spoon and drain on kitchen paper.

7. Serve the squid straight away with the dipping sauce and cucumber salad.

Sea trout with cucumber spaghetti, lemon butter sauce and horseradish potatoes

Trout, by which I mean sea trout not rainbow trout, is fairly easy to find, but this would be great with salmon, mackerel, or just about any fish. For the sauce to be good and creamy, the butter will need to be soft. If it's fridge hard, then just melt it: it'll still taste delicious.

Serves 2

140g (5oz) new potatoes (Jersey Royals are good)
2 sea trout fillets
½ lemon
85g (3oz) soft butter
½ cucumber
1 tsp horseradish sauce
a few sprigs of flat-leaf parsley or coriander

1. Put the kettle on to boil. Heat a heavy frying pan until very hot. Slice the potatoes as thick as a pound coin and cook them in a pan of boiling water (from the kettle) for 6–7 minutes.

2. Cook the trout fillets in the frying pan, turning once, until just done.

3. Squeeze the juice from ½ lemon and put it in a small pan. Boil until reduced to 2 tsp. Add a pinch of salt and beat the liquid into the butter (save 1 tsp for the potatoes) to make a mayonnaise-like sauce.

4. Peel the cucumber and use a vegetable peeler to make ribbons. Sprinkle with salt and squeeze dry in a tea towel. Heat 1 tbsp of the butter sauce in a pan and add the cucumber, stirring it into the butter. Cook until just hot through.

5. Drain the potatoes, stir in the remaining 1 tsp butter, the horseradish sauce and a few parsley or coriander leaves.

6. Pile the cucumber on a plate, top with the fish and pour over the sauce. Serve with the horseradish potatoes.

Salmon with pesto and prosciutto, flageolet beans and leeks in red wine

This way with salmon was sent to me by Kathryn Dashwood and it's one of the most popular '10 minutes to table' videos. Recipes using ovens are always tricky to tie to the 10 minute rule because they take variable amounts of time to warm up or, if you have an Aga, no time at all. If yours is a conventional oven, turn it on before you even take off your coat, to give it as much time as possible.

Serves 2

2 pieces of skinless salmon fillet
2 tbsp pesto
2 slices of prosciutto
1 large leek
olive oil
1–2 x 440g tins of flageolet beans
1 lemon
½ small glass of red wine

1. Preheat the oven to 200°C/400°F/Gas 6. Spread the salmon with pesto and wrap each piece in a slice of prosciutto. Pop the fish onto a baking sheet and bake for 8 minutes until just cooked through.

2. Slice the leek (throw away the dark green bit) into pieces and put into a bowl of water. Swish them around a bit, so that the dirt falls to the bottom. Heat 2 tbsp olive oil in a pan (with a lid). Scoop the leeks from the top of the bowl and put into the pan. Stir, cover and cook for 4 minutes.

3. Open the tin(s) of flageolet beans, drain and rinse. Put into a pan with a slug of olive oil and plenty of sea salt. Grate in the zest of a lemon. Heat through.

4. Add the wine to the leek pan and simmer uncovered for 1–2 minutes.

5. Season the beans with salt, pepper and a squeeze of lemon juice. Dollop onto two plates. Top each with a piece of salmon, and spoon the leeks alongside.

A few minutes less: Instead of the leeks in red wine, eat the salmon with steamed broccoli.

Speedy fish soup

This dish is a particular favourite of Loyd Grossman, my co-presenter on the '10 minutes to table' videos. He can't quite believe it's ready so quickly, when it tastes so sophisticated. Neither can I, but there it is.

Serves 2

1 leek
30g (1oz) butter
fat pinch of saffron
¼ bottle of white wine (nothing heavily oaked)
a dozen (or so) mussels
about 350g (12oz) mixed fish fillets (salmon and pollack are good)
3 tbsp crème fraîche
6 raw prawns
few sprigs of chervil or flat-leaf parsley
3 tbsp harissa or rouille
toast or crostini, to serve

1. Put the kettle on to boil. Slice the leek and wash it.

2. Melt the butter in a small pan (with a lid) and add the leeks. Stir, cover and leave to cook over a medium heat for 5 minutes.

3. Crumble the saffron into ½ teacupful of boiling water.

4. Put the wine in a pan and boil hard until reduced by half. Pour in the saffron and its liquid.

5. Clean the mussels, rejecting any which feel too heavy, are damaged or don't shut when firmly tapped on the sink. Pull off the beards. Rinse quickly. Add the mussels to the pan and cover. Cook for 1 minute or so until the mussels open. Throw away any shells that remain shut. Meanwhile, cut the fish into good-sized chunks.

6. Pour 300ml (½ pint) of boiling water into the leek pan and stir in the crème fraîche. Add the fish and prawns and simmer gently for 1–2 minutes until almost cooked.

7. Stir in the mussels and any juices in the pan. Taste and add seasoning, then scatter with the chervil or parsley leaves. Dot on the harissa or rouille and spread the rest on the toast or crostini and serve with the soup.

A few minutes less: Use a jar of good fish soup (French brands are often the best) and bring to just below simmering point. Add chunks of fish, mussels, or prawns and heat for 3 minutes, or until just cooked through. Top with a good dollop of crème fraîche and chopped chives, and eat with crusty bread.

A few minutes more: Add some sliced, boiled new potatoes at the same time as the crème fraîche.

Spinach and Parmesan pancakes with smoked haddock

With Pancake Day in mind, I've allowed enough batter to make some sweet pancakes for pudding, to eat with sugar and lemon. But if you don't have a sweet tooth, just make up the whole batch as savoury pancakes. Any unused batter will keep for 24 hours in the fridge.

Serves 2

4 tbsp butter
225ml (8fl oz) milk (any kind will do)
1 egg
4 dsp plain flour, heaped teeteringly high (about 110g/4oz)
1 large bag of washed fresh spinach (about 375g)
1 small piece of smoked haddock (about 110g/4oz)
hunk of Parmesan, enough to grate 2 tbsp
½ x 250g tub of ricotta
nutmeg
12 ripe cherry tomatoes

1. Put the kettle on to boil. Melt the butter in a large pan (with a lid).

2. Measure out the milk, add the egg, flour and a fat pinch of salt into a jug. Spoon in 2 tbsp of the melted butter and blitz briefly with a hand blender until smooth.

3. Add the spinach to the butter pan (save a handful to serve) with a pinch of salt, cover and cook over a medium heat for 2 minutes, stirring occasionally until the spinach wilts.

4. Put the fish in a bowl or pan, pour over enough boiling water to cover and put a lid on.

5. Pour half the batter into a separate bowl (this could be used for sweet pancakes) and add a few of the wilted spinach leaves to the remaining pancake batter. Grate in 2 tbsp Parmesan and blitz again with a hand blender until pale green.

6. Heat a heavy frying pan until very hot, add a tiny bit of butter and swirl it around. It will go brown, but don't worry. Pour in a small ladleful of batter and tip the pan so that it coats the base with a very thin layer, no thicker than the cover of a paperback. Tip out any excess mixture. Cook the pancake until browned underneath (use a fish slice to peek) and then flip over and cook on the other side, then slide out onto a plate and keep warm. Cook the rest of the pancakes in the same way.

7. Flake the fish and mix into the spinach pan with the ricotta, plus a good grating of nutmeg. Heat through gently. Use the mixture to fill the pancakes, and serve straight away with some halved cherry tomatoes and a handful of spinach leaves.

Poach the fish
then make
the batter

Pour hot water over the fish and cover

Add a little spinach to half the batter and blitz

Drain the fish and flake

Mix up filling
and roll the
pancakes

Cook the pancake until browned, then flip over

Spinach and Parmesan pancakes with smoked haddock

Blitz the milk, egg, flour, salt and butter until smooth

Melt the butter in a pan and add the spinach

Pour a small ladleful of batter into a very hot pan

Wilt the spinach and cook the pancakes

Mix the fish with the spinach, ricotta and nutmeg

Fill the pancake with the fish mixture and roll

Smoked haddock with crème fraîche and chives, Puy lentils and citrus broccoli

Smoked haddock, chives and crème fraîche are a great combination. If you prefer, boiled potatoes (sliced thinly so they'll cook in the time) and wilted spinach would be a good alternative to the lentils and broccoli.

Serves 2

280–340g (10–12oz) smoked haddock, skin on
milk (any kind will do)
1 small head of broccoli
butter
1 lemon or lime
1 x 250g sachet or tin of cooked Puy lentils
140ml (5fl oz) crème fraîche
1 clove of garlic
small bunch of chives
cornflour (optional)

1. Put the haddock skin side up in a saucepan and barely cover with milk. Poach the fish until the skin can be easily peeled away. Lift out of the milk, peel off the skin and keep the fish to one side.

2. Meanwhile, cut the broccoli into florets and steam or boil until just done, then toss in butter. Grate over a little lemon or lime zest. Heat the lentils through (drain and rinse first if from a tin) and add 1 tbsp crème fraîche and crush in the garlic.

3. Chop the chives and add to the remaining crème fraîche in a small pan. Heat gently and add a little of the fish cooking liquor, which is full of flavour but can be a bit salty. (The sauce will be quite thin, but if you prefer you could thicken it with 1 tsp cornflour.)

4. Pour the sauce over the fish and serve with the lentils and the broccoli.

Mussels with coconut, chilli and lemon grass

A bowl of mussels is fast and feels like holiday food, somehow special. I'm convinced it's largely down to eating with your fingers, which is slightly taboo, and so very sexy. Think of this as an Oriental moules marinière, with chilli and ginger balancing the sweetness of the shellfish.

Serves 2

olive oil
bunch of spring onions
piece of fresh ginger, peeled
¼ tsp turmeric
1 red chilli
1 small glass of white wine
1 stick of lemon grass or 1 lemon leaf
1 bag of mussels (about 1kg/2lb 4oz)
small bunch of fresh coriander, leaves chopped
½ x 400g tin of coconut milk

1. Heat a splash of oil in a large pan (with a lid) over a medium heat. Slice the spring onions and add to the pan with a good grating of fresh ginger and the turmeric. Slice enough of the chilli to give a good kick (taste a scrap to see how strong it is) and add that too.

2. Fry the onions gently. Meanwhile, clean the mussels, throwing out any which feel too heavy, are damaged or don't shut when firmly tapped against the sink. Pull off the beards. Rinse quickly.

3. Add a glass of wine to the onion pan and let it bubble up. Bash the stick of lemon grass with a rolling pin to bruise it, or use a fresh lemon leaf (the kind that sometimes comes attached to Italian lemons). Chuck in the mussels, cover the pan and give it a good shake.

4. Cook for 3 minutes or so until the mussel shells have opened. Throw away any shells that remain closed.

5. Meanwhile, chop the coriander leaves.

6. Add the coconut milk to the mussels, bring to simmering point, taste and adjust the seasoning. Sprinkle with coriander and serve straight away with napkins and a large bowl for the shells.

Ceviche of salmon with avocado and red onion

Raw fish 'cooked' in the acid of lime juice is a South American classic, blissfully easy to make, and a great starter or light lunch. The longer you leave the fish the more opaque and cooked it becomes, so don't hang around more than half an hour, say, before tucking in.

Serves 2

about 225g (8oz) very fresh, skinless salmon fillet
1 lime
½ small red onion
1 ripe avocado
1 red chilli

1. Slice the salmon as thinly as possible and lay the slices in a single layer over a large plate. Grate over some of the lime zest (use a zester if you have one): about ½ lime should be enough. Cut the lime in half and squeeze half the juice over the salmon, making sure all the fish is 'limed'.

2. Peel and slice the onion very thinly and scatter the rings over the fish.

3. Cut the avocado in half and remove the stone. With a blunt knife, cut the flesh into slices, cutting down to, but not through, the skin. Scoop out the flesh with a spoon, and arrange the slices over the fish and onion. Slice the red chilli and scatter over the ceviche plate. Squeeze over the rest of the lime juice, scatter with sea salt and serve.

5
minutes
to table

Smoked salmon and chive chowder with chilli crème fraîche

There's something very comforting about milk-based soups like this chowder. It's the hot-milk effect, I suppose. If you have some leftover cooked potatoes in the fridge, then add them to the soup to make it extra sustaining.

Serves 2

500ml (a scant 1 pint) milk (any kind will do)
300ml tub of chicken stock
handful of frozen sweetcorn kernels
small bunch of chives
3 slices of smoked salmon or the equivalent of smoked salmon scraps
2 tbsp crème fraîche or sour cream
a few drops of chilli sauce

1. Put the milk and stock in a pan and add the sweetcorn kernels. Chop the chives and roughly chop the smoked salmon.

2. Bring to simmering point and stir in the salmon. Cook for a few seconds, then add the chopped chives.

3. Stir the crème fraîche or sour cream with enough chilli sauce to make it nice and spicy.

4. Serve the soup with a dollop of crème fraîche on top of each bowlful.

5
minutes
to table

Seared tuna with lime lentils and a soy dipping sauce

The mild flavour of fresh tuna is great with the lime-spiked lentils. Don't cook the tuna right through or it will be dry and tough. If it must be well done, then save money and time by buying a tin of tuna instead: it'll taste better. Look for sustainably caught yellowfin tuna.

Serves 2

1 tuna steak (about 225g/8oz)
olive oil
1–2 x 400g tins or sachets of cooked lentils (Puy lentils if possible)
2 limes
½ small red onion
½ cucumber
4 tbsp Japanese soy sauce
wasabi paste (optional)

1. Heat a heavy frying pan or a griddle until very hot. Rub the tuna steak with oil and cook for 1–2 minutes each side, so only the outside 0.5cm (¼ inch) of the steak is cooked. Sprinkle with salt and put to one side.

2. Drain the lentils (rinse them if they were tinned – the ones in sachets don't need it) and heat gently in a small pan.

3. Take the zest off 1 lime with a zester and mix into the lentils, along with a slug of olive oil. Peel and chop the onion finely and mix in. Halve the lime and squeeze in the juice – taste as you go, you may not need it all. Season with salt.

4. Cut the other lime in half. Thinly slice the cucumber.

5. Mix the soy sauce with a pea-sized blob of wasabi, if you are using it, and pour into two tiny dishes (tea-light holders work well, as long as they are food safe).

6. Slice the seared tuna thinly. Arrange the lentils on two plates and top with the tuna. Add the lime, cucumber and a little bowl of the soy dipping sauce. Serve extra wasabi if you like.

10 : Veg

minutes
to table

Asparagus with buffalo mozzarella, pine nuts, peas and new potatoes

At the risk of sounding dictatorial, the first English asparagus of the year should always be eaten with melted butter or (for the fancier cook) hollandaise sauce. But once the season is in full swing, there's room for a less purist approach. Try it in this salad, a sort of homage to early summer.

Serves 2

100g (3½oz) tiny new potatoes (Jersey Royals are best)
large bunch of English asparagus
handful of fresh peas in their pods
3 tbsp pine nuts
handful of wild rocket
ball of buffalo mozzarella
for the dressing:
4 tbsp olive oil
1 tbsp lemon or lime juice

1. Put the kettle on to boil and fill a pan with the boiling water. Wash the potatoes, slice into halves or quarters and add to the pan. Boil for about 7 minutes until cooked.

2. Peel the bottom 7.5cm (3 inches) or so of the asparagus with a vegetable peeler and put into a steamer over the potatoes. Steam for 4–5 minutes until tender (not crunchy).

3. Quickly pod the peas and add to the steamer for the last 3–4 minutes.

4. Put the pine nuts in a dry frying pan and toast until lightly browned.

5. Whisk the dressing ingredients together and season with salt and pepper. Drain the potatoes and mix with the asparagus, peas, rocket and the dressing. Arrange on a plate. Rip the mozzarella and chuck it on top. Scatter on the pine nuts and serve.

Asparagus with poached duck egg and Parmesan wafers

A satisfyingly simple way to serve new season English asparagus. Duck eggs have a gloriously rich orange yolk, but use a hen's egg, or any egg, if that's easier. The Parmesan wafers are a great trick, easy to make, very impressive looking, and addictive to eat. Make them by themselves to nibble with pre-dinner drinks.

Serves 2

large bunch of English asparagus
2 duck eggs
hunk of Parmesan, big enough to grate 4 tbsp
1 tbsp butter

1. Put a full kettle on to boil. Heat a heavy frying pan or smooth griddle and line with a heatproof silicone liner if you have one.

2. Trim the bottom of the asparagus. Using half the water from the kettle, steam the asparagus in a steamer, or boil it in a wide frying pan, for about 4 minutes, until just done.

3. Meanwhile, put the rest of the boiling water into a large pan (with a lid) and boil again. Break the eggs into the pan (one each side), and lower the heat so the water is barely simmering. Cover and leave for 5 minutes until just set. Lift out the poached eggs, one at a time, with a slotted spoon, patting each dry with kitchen paper.

4. Grate 4 tbsp Parmesan and sprinkle it in four circles on the hot silicone liner (or the bare pan). Watch carefully as the cheese melts. When the wafers turn caramel brown at the edges, lift the liner out of the pan to cool (or use a fish slice to lift out the Parmesan wafers).

5. Toss the hot asparagus in the butter and arrange on two plates. Top with the poached eggs and Parmesan wafers .

A few minutes less: Don't make the Parmesan wafers but eat this with thin slices of toast instead.

Tomato, soft cheese and sesame tart

The thing about a tart like this, is that you can put whatever you like on top. Raid the deli counter for grilled peppers, roast aubergines, artichokes and the like, but do check that the vegetables aren't vinegary before you buy them.

Serves 2

½ x 375g pack of ready-rolled puff pastry
2 tbsp sesame seeds
200g (7oz) Brie or other soft cheese
300g (10½oz) cherry tomatoes on the vine
for the parsley, caper and olive pesto:
bunch of flat-leaf parsley
1 tbsp small capers
handful of olives (black, green or a mixture)
olive oil

1. Preheat the oven to 450°F/220°C/Gas 8 and put a large baking sheet in to heat.

2. Lay the pastry on a piece of baking parchment. Sprinkle the pastry with the sesame seeds (making sure they go right to the edge) and roll out the pastry to half its original thickness, pressing in the sesame seeds with the rolling pin. Trim the edges to make a neat rectangle.

3. With a sharp knife, score a border around the edge about 2cm (1 inch) wide, being careful not to cut all the way through the pastry. Lift the pastry, still on the baking parchment, onto the hot baking sheet and bake for 2 minutes, while you get everything else ready.

4. Slice the Brie thinly. Take the pastry out of the oven and lay the cheese over it (not on the border), then arrange the tomatoes on top. Bake for 7 minutes, until browned and crisp.

5. Rip the leaves off the parsley and chop fairly small. Place in a mortar with the capers. Stone and chop the olives and add those too. Add a good glug of oil, enough to make a pesto-like consistency. Stir well, then taste and season with sea salt. Drizzle the pesto over the tart when it comes out of the oven. Serve straight away, pulling off the tomato stalks as you eat.

A few minutes less: Buy a ready-made, large, savoury tart case, spread the base thickly with crème fraîche and arrange the rest of the tart's ingredients on top. Sprinkle with sesame seeds and bake until hot through.

Roll out the pastry
and get it in
the oven

Sprinkle pastry with sesame seeds and roll out

Slice the cheese thinly

Place the cheese on the part-baked pastry

Mix up the pesto

Combine the parsley, capers and olives

Tomato, soft cheese and sesame tart

Trim the edges and score a border around the edge

Put the pastry onto a tray, bake for 2 minutes

Cover with tomatoes and bake for 7 minutes

Add the cheese and tomatoes

Add olive oil and mix to a pesto-like consistency

Remove tart from oven and drizzle with pesto

Spicy, creamy tomato soup

Don't automatically leave out the chilli if you are making this for children. They often love it.

Serves 2

1 tbsp butter
1 clove of garlic, peeled
1 x 400g tin of tomatoes
1 tbsp tomato purée
shake of chilli sauce (sweet chilli sauce works well)
2 tbsp cream (single, double, whipping or even crème fraîche)
nutmeg

1. Melt the butter in a small pan. Slice the garlic and add it to the pan.

2. As the garlic cooks, open the tin of tomatoes. Tip into the pan, along with the tomato purée, a mugful of water (around 225ml/8fl oz if you're measuring, but accuracy is not really the point here), and shake in some chilli sauce.

3. As it heats, whiz it with a hand blender until smooth. Don't let the mixture boil if you can avoid it.

4. Stir in 1 tbsp cream, season with salt and pepper, and grate in a good bit of nutmeg. Serve with the rest of the cream dribbled on top.

5
minutes
to table

Pea and mint soup

A pretty, bright green soup for spring or anytime. If you're particularly hungry, make a cheese sandwich with a hard British cheese, like Cheshire, Wensleydale or decent Cheddar, to eat with it.

Serves 2

1 tbsp butter
3 spring onions
300g (11oz) frozen or fresh podded peas
3 tbsp cream cheese
3 sprigs of mint

1. Put the kettle on to boil. Melt the butter in a large pan, slice the spring onions and let them sizzle away for 1–2 minutes.

2. Put the peas in a pan over a high heat and pour over about 400ml (¾ pint) boiling water (or stock, if you have it). Bring to the boil. Scoop out a couple of spoonfuls of peas, then pour the rest of the peas with all their water into the spring onion pan.

3. Add half the cream cheese and the mint leaves to the soup, and blitz with a hand blender until smooth and frothy.

4. Mix the rest of the cream cheese with 2 tbsp hot water to make a smooth cream. Taste the soup and season with salt and pepper, then pour into two bowls. Add the reserved peas, swirl the cream cheese on top and serve.

Gazpacho with olive and goats' cheese toasts

A sort of liquid salad for a hot, hot day. Some recipes add bread to the mix, which makes for a more substantial soup, but one with a peculiar salmon colour. I prefer this vividly coloured, refreshing version.

Serves 2–4

for the gazpacho:
½ cucumber
2 spring onions
1 tiny clove of garlic, peled
1 small red or yellow pepper
500g (1lb) really ripe tomatoes
1 tsp sherry vinegar
scrap of chilli or a little chilli sauce
1 tbsp olive oil, plus extra to drizzle over
for the goats' cheese toasts:
½ teacupful of olives
6 slices of ciabatta
olive oil
small round of soft goats' cheese or goats' cheese log
1 tbsp capers
4 sprigs of basil

1. Peel and chop the cucumber, onions, garlic and pepper. Purée all the gazpacho ingredients in a blender until as smooth as possible. Serve with ice cubes and a drizzle of olive oil.

2. Pit the olives. Toast the ciabatta and drizzle with olive oil. Spread with the goats' cheese and scatter over the olives and capers. Rip the basil leaves and scatter them over the toasts, too.

Pea and herb frittata with a goats' cheese cream and tomato salad

This slim frittata (it has to be slender or it won't cook in time) is as good cold as warm, making it a great lunchbox filler.

Serves 2

small bunch of dill
small bunch of flat-leaf parsley
small bunch of chives
1 teacupful of frozen peas or podded fresh peas
4 eggs
butter
3 ripe tomatoes
2 tbsp soft goats' cheese
6 tbsp Greek yoghurt

1. Put the kettle on to boil. Heat a 20cm (8 inch) heavy frying pan and the grill until both are very hot. Chop the dill, parsley and a couple of the chives. Put the peas in a bowl and pour over boiling water.

2. Lightly beat the eggs, add the herbs and season. Then drain the peas and add those too. Melt a good knob of butter in the frying pan and when it is foaming pour in the eggs.

3. Slice the tomatoes and sprinkle with salt, a tiny bit of sugar and pepper.

4. Beat the goats' cheese and yoghurt together until smooth. Chop the remaining chives and add those too, keeping a few to sprinkle over the top.

5. Once the frittata is set and golden on the bottom, pop it under the hot grill to finish the top (or use a blow torch).

6. Serve the frittata hot or cold – it will set more as it cools – with the goats' cheese cream and the tomato salad.

Edamame peas with soy, broccoli, coriander and noodles

Great for lunchboxes. Do make sure you drain the noodles really well, or the dressing will be watered down, and don't resort to the 'straight to wok' noodles, which taste weird. Chilli heads may like to add a chopped green chilli for extra heat.

Serves 2

110g (4oz) egg noodles
1 teacupful of edamame peas
1 head of broccoli or a pack of 'tenderstem' broccoli
2 tbsp light soy sauce
2 tbsp toasted sesame oil
½ lime
0.5cm (¼ inch) piece of fresh ginger, peeled
2 spring onions
handful of fresh coriander

1. Pul the kettle on to boil. Put the edamame peas in a bowl and cover with boiling water.

2. Cook the noodles according to the instructions on the pack, until just done but still springy.

3. Cut the broccoli into short lengths (the stems of tenderstem broccoli can be eaten too) and steam over the noodles until bright green and still a bit crunchy.

4. Drain the noodles, cool under a cold tap, and drain again thoroughly. Put in a bowl.

5. Whisk the soy sauce and sesame oil together. Squeeze in the lime juice and grate in the zest. Grate in the ginger. Pour the dressing over the noodles, turning to coat them well.

6. Slice the spring onions, chop the coriander and add to the bowl along with the drained edamame peas and broccoli. Mix well, taste to check the seasoning, adding a little more sesame oil or soy if you like.

Spinach with pine nuts and raisins

This is a Spanish classic, good on its own or as part of a collection of dishes served tapas style. I'm assuming you are going to use a bag of ready-washed spinach, but by all means use unwashed, just rip out any tough stalks as you wash it.

Serves 2

2 tbsp olive oil
3 anchovy fillets in olive oil (optional)
1 clove of garlic, peeled
2 tbsp plump, juicy raisins
1 large bag of fresh spinach (about 300g)
2 tbsp toasted pine nuts
nutmeg
dollop of Greek yoghurt

1. Heat the oil in a large pan over a medium-high heat. Chop the anchovies, if you are using them, and add to the pan.

2. Crush in the garlic, add a pinch of salt and the plump raisins, then pile in the spinach. Stir in the hot oil until the spinach wilts, keeping the heat high to evaporate as much of the liquid as possible.

3. Stir in the pine nuts and grate over a bit of nutmeg. Taste and add salt and pepper, then pile into a bowl and serve with a dollop of Greek yoghurt.

5
minutes
to table

Couscous with harissa, rocket and goats' cheese

About 15 years ago Delia Smith brought out the first in the new wave of seasonal cookbooks, called the *Summer Collection*. It was a huge bestseller, and for a while no lunch party was complete without her couscous and roasted vegetable salad. Delia's recipes have gone in and out of fashion since then, but that salad remains an outstandingly good dish. This is my 5 minute homage to Delia.

Serves 2

1 teacupful of couscous
2 tsp harissa
2 tbsp tomato purée
1 slice of a large goats' cheese log
handful of wild rocket

1. Put the kettle on to boil, put the couscous in a bowl with a pinch of salt and pour over a teacupful of water. Cover and leave to one side for 4 minutes.

2. Mix the harissa with the tomato purée and stir in enough hot water (about 3 tbsp) to make a sauce. (I use Belazu's harissa, which is not very hot. With other brands you may need less.)

3. Crumble or dice the goats' cheese.

4. Fork up the couscous and taste to check the seasoning. Mix in the rocket and goats' cheese and pile on plates. Drizzle over the harissa sauce and serve straight away.

5
minutes
to table

Mezze with homemade thyme flatbread

A bright, flavoured mix of Lebanese-style mezze. And yes, I know, tabbouleh should be made with bulghur wheat, not couscous. But this fast version respects the crucial rule, that the main ingredient should be the herbs.

Serves 2

for the tabbouleh:
4 tbsp couscous
2 ripe tomatoes
small bunch each of flat-leaf parsley and mint, leaves only
2 spring onions, trimmed
1 tbsp lemon juice, or to taste
3 tbsp extra-virgin olive oil
pomegranate seeds, to scatter over (optional)
for the flatbread:
teacupful of self-raising flour (110g/4oz)
1 tbsp olive oil
5 sprigs of thyme
2 tbsp pumpkin seeds (sunflower seeds work well too)
for the tarator:
4 tbsp tahini
juice of ½ lemon, or to taste
1 clove of garlic, peeled
to serve:
Labneh or feta cheese, drizzled with oil, and with a little lemon zest grated over
1 little gem lettuce (divided into leaves), carrot slices, cucumber sticks and radishes

1. Put the kettle on to boil. Pour 4 tbsp boiling water over the couscous, cover and leave for 5 minutes.

2. Dice the tomatoes, finely chop the herbs and slice the spring onions very thinly. Add with the lemon juice and oil to the couscous. Season well and scatter with pomegranate seeds.

3. Heat a dry frying pan or griddle until very hot. Mix the flour with a fat pinch of salt, the olive oil and enough water (about 4 tbsp) to make a stiff dough. Add the thyme leaves.

4. Divide the dough in two and roll out no more than pencil thick. Scatter over the seeds and roll them in. Cook the breads for about 2 minutes on each side, until well browned.

5. Put the tahini in a bowl and stir in the lemon juice. Then add water, spoonful by spoonful. It will go stiff at first and then thin down to a creamy consistency. Crush in the garlic and season with salt. Taste and add a bit more lemon juice if you like.

6. Arrange the tarator, tabbouleh, cheese and flatbread on a platter with the lettuce and vegetables, and serve.

Little courgette pancakes with sweetcorn and chives

These yummy little pancakes – a sort of courgette rösti meets old-fashioned drop scone – are inspired by a recipe sent in to The *Daily Telegraph* 'Readers' Recipes' column years ago. Vegetarians could eat them with just the tomato salad.

Serves 2

2 corn on the cob (the 'supersweet' kind)
4–6 rashers of smoked streaky bacon
1 x 15cm (6 inch) courgette
30g (1oz) Cheddar cheese
2 spring onions, chopped
2 tbsp self-raising flour
1 egg, beaten
olive oil or butter
2 ripe tomatoes
2 tbsp crème fraîche
small bunch of chives

1. Put the kettle on to boil. Cut the corn into slices as thick as a finger. Pour the boiling water into a pan, add the corn and cook for 5 minutes until done.

2. Meanwhile, heat a large heavy frying pan and cook the bacon until browned and crisp.

3. Coarsely grate the courgette and the cheese, then mix with the spring onions, flour and egg. Season well with salt and pepper. Heat a large, heavy frying pan with a little oil or butter until hot. Place heaped tablespoons of mixture in the pan and cook for 2½ minutes until brown. Turn over and cook the other side for a further 2½ minutes.

4. Slice the tomatoes and sprinkle with salt and pepper and a little olive oil.

5. Drain the sweetcorn and mix with the crème fraiche and snip over the chives.

6. Serve the pancakes with the sweetcorn, tomato salad and bacon.

Homemade pasta with garlic, chilli and rocket

Homemade pasta is worth the trouble, with a flavour and texture that outclasses factory-made fresh pasta. With the help of a food processor and a pasta machine, it can, amazingly, be made in less time than it takes many dried pastas to cook. And once you have the hang of the technique, you can add flavourings, chopped herbs, chilli, even saffron, to the dough.

If you don't have a pasta machine, or want to save a few minutes, use good-quality dried pasta instead. It is generally better than mass-produced fresh pasta, but do check the label that it will cook in 5 minutes or less. Cipriani, beautifully packaged like a bottle of expensive perfume, is a pricey but excellent brand.

Serves 2

teacupful of strong white flour (100g/4oz)
1 egg
4 tbsp extra-virgin olive oil
1 red chilli
1 clove of garlic, peeled
2 handfuls of wild rocket
60g (2oz) soft goats' cheese or freshly grated Parmesan

1. Put a large pan half full of water on to boil, and boil the kettle (this is to reduce the time it takes to get a large panful of water to boil). Put the flour in a food processor and whiz together with the egg to make a crumbly dough.

2. Knead for a moment or two then press into a flat oval. Put through the widest setting of the pasta machine, fold in three and repeat. Repeat a couple more times until the dough feels smooth. Reduce the setting on the pasta machine by one notch, and put the dough through. Keep rolling the dough, reducing the setting each time. Cut the dough in half if it gets too long. Once it has gone through the finest setting, cut it into tagliatelle on the purpose-made cutter.

3. By now the water should be boiling – top it up with the water from the kettle. Add 1 tsp salt and the pasta and cook for 2 minutes or so, until just done.

4. Meanwhile, heat 4 tbsp olive oil gently in a small pan. Slice the chilli (throw away the seeds if you don't want it too hot) and garlic and add to the pan. Cook gently for 1–2 minutes.

5. Scoop a bit of the pasta water into a cup. Drain the rest of the water from the pasta and toss in the hot garlic-chilli oil with 2 tbsp pasta water. Mix in the rocket and crumbled goats' cheese or Parmesan, and a fat pinch of sea salt. Pile on plates and eat straight away.

Ricotta, spring vegetables and tarragon pasta

I love tarragon, but it can vary wildly in flavour from the mild to the overpoweringly aniseedy. This is especially true of plants in the garden, which can be either the pungent Russian tarragon or the light-flavoured French variety (the sort usually sold in greengrocers and supermarkets).

If I happen to have some other spring vegetables, a few foraged leaves of wild garlic, say, or some baby chard, I would certainly add them, either with the tarragon (for delicate leaves) or with the peas (for more robust veg).

Serves 2

225g (8oz) dried tagliatelle or vermicelli (check the pack that it cooks in 4 minutes
  or less. Cipriani is a good brand to look for)
1 courgette
½ teacupful of frozen or fresh peas
2 heaped tbsp ricotta
hunk of Parmesan, big enough to grate 1 tbsp
6 sprigs of tarragon
½ lime
1 tbsp extra-virgin olive oil

1. Put the kettle on to boil, heat a saucepan and pour in the boiling water. Bring back to the boil, add 1 tsp salt and the pasta.

2. With a vegetable peeler, quickly cut a pile of ribbons from the courgette.

3. About 1 minute before the pasta is done, add the peas and scoop out 2 tbsp pasta water. Continue boiling until the pasta is barely done, adding the courgette ribbons for just the last 5 seconds.

4. Meanwhile, mix the pasta water with the ricotta and grate in about 1 tbsp Parmesan. Drain the pasta, peas and courgettes, mix with the ricotta cream and rip in the tarragon leaves.

5. Taste and check the seasoning, squeezing in a little lime juice if it needs it. Pile into two deep bowls, sprinkle with olive oil and serve.

5
minutes
to table

Beetroot soup with horseradish cream

A vividly coloured, warm bowlful. Check the beetroot pack to make sure that it doesn't contain vinegar.

Serves 2

1 tbsp olive oil
1 clove of garlic, peeled
1 x 250g vacuum pack of cooked beetroot
1 x 400g tin of tomatoes
to serve:
1 tbsp crème fraîche
½ tsp horseradish sauce (or creamed horseradish)
1 tbsp chopped herbs – dill, flat-leaf parsley, chives, chervil or coriander (optional)

1. Put the oil in a small pan over a medium heat and crush in the garlic.

2. Chop one of the smaller beetroot into little chunks and set aside. Add the rest of the beetroot and the tomatoes to the pan, plus about ⅓ tinful of water.

3. While it heats, whiz the mixture smooth with a hand blender. Taste and season with salt and pepper. The soup should be piping hot but not boiling. Stir in the chopped beetroot.

4. Mix the crème fraîche with the horseradish and serve in dollops on the soup. Sprinkle over some chopped herbs if you have them.

5
minutes
to table

Pappardelle with mushrooms, rosemary and lemon crumbs

Zesty fried crumbs give a great texture to pasta dishes. This is a good dish for a mixed table of vegetarians and non-vegetarians because the mushrooms taste surprisingly meaty.

Serves 2

3 tbsp butter
340g (12oz) portobello or open-cup mushrooms
sprig of rosemary
225g (8oz) pappardelle
1 slice of good bread
1 clove of garlic, peeled
1 lemon
small bunch of flat-leaf parsley

1. Put the kettle on to boil.

2. Meanwhile, melt 1 tbsp butter in a heavy frying pan (one with a lid).Cut the mushrooms into four, if large, and turn in the butter, adding a pinch of salt. Chop the rosemary and add that too. Cover and cook over a medium-high heat for 3 minutes (to wilt the mushrooms slightly) then take the lid off and continue cooking.

3. Pour the boiling water into a large pan, add 1 tsp salt and the pasta. Cook the pappardelle following the instructions on the packet until just *al dente*. Drain, reserving a teacupful of pasta water.

4. While the pasta is cooking, cut the crusts off the bread and whiz into breadcrumbs in a small food processor.

5. In another frying pan, melt 1 tbsp butter and add the crumbs. Crush in the garlic. Cook the crumbs until crisp and brown. Grate in a little lemon zest (about ¼ lemon) and chop the parsley, stirring that in, too, off the heat.

6. Mix the pasta with the mushrooms, adding a splash of the pasta water to loosen the juices caramelized on the bottom of the pan. Stir in the last of the butter.

7. Serve the mushroom pasta in a wide bowl with the crumbs scattered over.

Homemade tortillas with guacamole, refried beans and mango salsa

A real Mexican feast is tight in 10 minutes, but it can be done.

Serves 2

for the flour tortillas:
teacupful of self-raising flour (about 110g/4oz)
1 tsp lard or vegetable oil
5 tbsp warm water
for the refried beans:
2 tbsp lard or vegetable oil
3 spring onions
1 x 400g tin of pinto or red kidney beans
small matchbox-sized piece of Cheshire or Wensleydale cheese
for the guacamole:
1 ripe avocado
juice of 1 lime
½ red chilli
1 clove of garlic, peeled
for the mango salsa:
1 ripe mango
½ red chilli
1 lime
to serve:
sour cream

1. Mix the flour, oil or lard and 5 tbsp water in a mini food processor with a pinch of salt. Heat a heavy frying pan until very hot. Divide the mixture into four and roll out into thin circles on a floured surface. Cook one at a time, for ½–1 minute each side, just until set, not brown.

2. Heat the lard or oil in a pan until sizzling. Slice the spring onions and add to the pan. Drain and rinse the tinned beans. Add to the pan, mash the beans and stir well to give a creamy texture. When hot, taste and season with salt. Crumble over the cheese.

3. Halve the avocado and mash the flesh with a fork. Scoop into a bowl, squeeze in the lime juice and a pinch of salt. Chop the chilli finely and add to the mix. Crush in a garlic clove.

4. Slice the 'cheeks' of mango from each side of the stone. Score the flesh deeply (not cutting through the skin) in pencil-wide strips, then across in a grid. Use a spoon to scoop out the flesh, in pea-sized chunks, into a bowl. Chop the red chilli and mix in with a fat pinch of salt. Grate over a little lime zest and squeeze over the lime juice.

5. Serve the tortillas, beans, guacamole and salsa with a bowl of sour cream.

Make the tortilla dough first

Mix the flour and lard in a mini food processor

Heat the oil in a pan and add the spring onions

Mash the flesh of the avocado with a fork

Make the mango salsa

Mash the beans to a creamy texture and season

Homemade tortillas with guacamole, refried beans and mango salsa

Roll out the mixture into four thin circles

Cook one at a time in a hot frying pan until set

Rinse the beans and add to the spring onions

Get the beans
going and mash
the avocado

Slice the mango and mix in the chopped chilli

Crumble the cheese over the refried beans

Tuscan bean soup

A simple blend of vegetables and beans. I often add a shake of chilli sauce or a bit of chopped red chilli to spice it up.

Serves 2

2 tbsp olive oil, plus extra to drizzle
1 clove of garlic, peeled
4 sprigs of flat-leaf parsley
1 stick of celery
1 carrot
2 x 400g tins of borlotti beans or other beans
1 x 300ml tub of chicken stock or water

1. Heat the oil in a large saucepan and crush in the garlic.

2. Rip the leaves from 2 sprigs of parsley and roughly chop them together with the celery and carrot, then use a mini food processor to chop finely. Stir them into the pan too.

3. Cook for a moment, then add the drained and rinsed beans, stock, a fat pinch of salt and a tinful of water. Bring to simmering point, cook for 1 minute, then purée the soup roughly with a hand blender.

4. Taste and add salt and pepper, then ladle into bowls, drizzle with oil and rip over the rest of the parsley.

5
minutes
to table

Substantial bruschetta of haricot beans, lemon and chilli

Zingy with chilli and lemon, these are Formula One beans on toast: stylish and wickedly fast.

Serves 2

1 x 400g tin of cannellini beans, or haricot, or borlotti
1 small clove of garlic, peeled
2 thick slices of good bread (sourdough is best, but ciabatta will do)
extra-virgin olive oil
small bunch of flat-leaf parsley
½ lemon

1. Drain and rinse the beans quickly and tip into a pan. Add ½ tinful of cold water and crush in the garlic.

2. Heat through. Meanwhile, toast the bread and trickle a little olive oil over it.

3. Roughly chop the parsley. Flavour the beans with a squeeze of lemon juice, and grate in a little of the zest. Stir in a glug of olive oil, salt and pepper and most of the parsley.

4. Taste and adjust the seasoning, then pile onto the hot toast. Scatter with the rest of the parsley and eat straight away.

5
minutes
to table

Smoky cheese fondue

Fondue is one of those dishes that makes people misty eyed with nostalgia – and it's so easy to make. You don't even need a fondue set, although if you got married in the eighties you probably got one as a wedding present. Improvise with a saucepan and ordinary forks otherwise, popping the pan back on the heat and giving it a good stir if it gets a bit thick.

Serves 2

1 glass of dry white wine (about 140ml/5floz)
½ clove of garlic, peeled
225g (8oz) grated Swiss cheese (a mixture of Emmenthal and Gruyère works well)
2 tbsp flour
cubes of crusty bread, chunks of ham and vegetables, for dipping
1 tbsp Kirsch or brandy (optional)
hunk of Parmesan, big enough to grate 2 tbsp
nutmeg

1. Pour the white wine in a smallish pan, add the garlic and bring to a gentle simmer. Gently toss the Swiss cheese and flour together until the cheese is coated.

2. Chop the vegetables, bread and ham. Steam or boil any vegetables that need it – think about whether they'll be nice raw with cheese sauce.

3. Back to the simmering wine. Add the floury Swiss cheese to the pot a handful at a time, stirring all the time. When melted and smooth, add the Kirsch or brandy, if you are using it. Taste and grate in the Parmesan and a little nutmeg if it needs a bit more oomph – a lot depends on the cheese. Heat carefully, to just below boiling, stirring all the time.

4. Serve with bread cubes, chunks of ham and vegetables.

Fast ingredients

Meat

- **When it is vital that the ingredients cook right through,** cut them into small pieces, either little chunks or slender slices, to speed the process. So chicken breasts need to be sliced horizontally into two escalopes, and pork steaks should be no more than finger thick. Beef and lamb don't need cooking through, so provided you are happy with pink meat, both can be kept in larger pieces. Remember, rare steak is delicious, but lamb is generally best pink not bloody.
- **Resting time.** All meat is better given a little time to rest away from direct heat after cooking. For small pieces of meat, the kind used in this book, 5 minutes is plenty.
- **Be realistic.** Cheap cuts such as braising steak need long slow cooking to be good. Prime cuts, steak and chops for instance, tend to be the best bet for the fast cook, because they don't need time to tenderize. Cheaper cuts that cook in a flash include liver, boned-out chicken thighs and sliced lamb neck fillet. Save the bone-in cuts for when you have another 5 or 10 minutes.
- **Pressing down on a piece of meat** as it cooks compacts the flesh and encourages the heat to travel to the centre so that it cooks through faster.

Fish

- **Fish is perfect fast food,** because almost all fish will cook beautifully in 10 minutes. Don't forget shellfish, such as mussels, clams and scallops too.
- **Whole fish that are no thicker than your thumb** at the widest part should be done in 10 minutes, but larger fish will need filleting.
- **For the simplest sauce,** melt 2 tbsp salted butter and heat until golden. Squeeze in ½ small lemon and stir in 1 tbsp chopped herbs such as flat-leaf parsley, chives, chervil, dill.

Vegetables

- **Like fish, vegetables shouldn't present many problems**. Only a few (such as red cabbage) benefit from being cooked for longer than 10 minutes.
- **Cook delicate vegetables** in the minimum of water. Leaves such as spinach need no water at all.
- **Don't forget your grater.** Even strident swede is delicious grated and boiled for 7 minutes, drained and mixed with butter and lots of black pepper. Other grated veg can be cooked just in butter and their own juices.
- **Salad is a good standby,** but try not to grab a bag every time. Look for homegrown vegetables instead. Spring cabbage is quick to shred and can be eaten raw or cooked in seconds.
- **A vegetable peeler** cuts long ribbons of carrot, cucumber and courgette for salads or to wilt in a little hot butter. They look glamorous and taste great.

Potatoes and carbohydrates

Often the trickiest bit to do in 10 minutes. Here's a checklist of possibilities:

- **Tinned beans.** Cooking tinned beans is little more than rinsing and reheating in a pan. If you have time, start by frying bacon, or chorizo, or other cured pork, until the fat runs, before adding the beans. Or heat the beans with a splash of water and a dollop of olive oil (or butter, or duck fat). Either way, add plenty of salt. Stick a hand blender briefly into the pan to purée a few of the beans, then stir to bathe the rest in a creamy sauce. Organic beans are often tinned without salt, which means they collapse to a mush, fine if you want a purée.
- **Sachets or tins of cooked lentils.** These are a great fast supper, especially grey-brown, earthy-flavoured Puy lentils. Treat them in the same way as beans (see above), or cook with bacon and toss onto some robust salad leaves dressed with a balsamic vinegar vinaigrette for a fast warm salad.
- **Couscous.** Purists steam couscous for half an hour or more but it's fine to pour boiling water or stock over the fine grains, cover the bowl with a plate, and leave for 5 minutes. Then stir with a fork to fluff it up and serve. Remember, you need an equal volume of dry couscous to liquid, so 1 teacupful of couscous (plenty for two people) needs 1 teacupful of liquid.
- **Flatbread.** You can make homemade flatbread by mixing a teacupful of self-raising flour with a splash of olive oil, a fat pinch of salt and enough water to make a soft dough. Add flavourings such as chopped herbs or spices and knead for a few seconds until fairly smooth. Divide into two, roll out pencil thin and cook on a dry hot griddle or frying pan, for 2–3 minutes on each side.
- **Other bread.** Make sure it's a decent chewy loaf. Pitta bread and tortillas are both the fast cook's friends. Warming in a hot frying pan or griddle is generally quicker than heating the grill.
- **Rice.** It will never cook in the time. I use it when I'm not up against the clock. Sachets of ready-cooked rice are OK.
- **Soft polenta.** A northern Italian staple, it's ground cornmeal cooked with water to make a creamy buttercup-yellow mush, a speedy mashed potato alternative. I use quick-cook '1 minute' polenta. In fact, the mixture has to come up to boiling first, then simmer for 1 minute, so it's more like 4 minutes. One caveat, polenta's flavour is dull, so add plenty of salt, crushed garlic, grated Parmesan or chopped herbs to liven it up.
- **Firm polenta.** Sold vacuum-packed in blocks, it's just soft polenta, cooked until thick and left to cool into a firm slab, and very popular with Italians. It is a good storecupboard staple and can be relied on to cook without collapsing (unlike homemade polenta, which has an infuriating habit of reverting to mush). Brush with oil (crush in a clove of garlic first) and cook in a heavy frying pan, until lightly browned, or on a griddle for those pretty brown stripes.
- **Potatoes.** These will cook in time, but only if you slice them thinly (no more than pencil thick). Cook them in lots of salted boiling water, then toss them in butter or oil.
- **Other vegetables.** Don't forget that potatoes are not the only starch. A goodly helping of parsnips, peas or sweet potatoes, for instance, will do the same job.

Basic rules for fast food

- **Keep it simple**. Rediscover how good unfussy food can be.
- **Multitask.** Most of my 10 minute recipes will include phrases like 'meanwhile, do this' or 'while it simmers, do that'.
- **Be realistic.** Casseroles are slow-cook dishes. You are never going to make one in 10 minutes. Stick to grilling, frying, boiling and poaching.
- **As soon as you get into the kitchen, boil the kettle.** It helps to get the ball rolling, and you'll almost certainly need boiling water for something, if only a cup of tea.
- **Fast cooking needs fierce heat,** so your next job is to heat up the oven, griddle or pan that you'll be using.
- **Put your ingredients out** on the work surface before you start.
- **Assign a bowl for waste** where all the cooking detritus can go straight in.
- **Assess which item is going to take longest to cook** and get that underway.
- **Don't stop!** Even a few spare seconds can be used to wipe down a surface, sweep wrappers into the bin or chop some herbs.
- **A very hot pan means just that.** If you flick a few drops of water into the pan they will sizzle and skid and evaporate almost immediately; oil in a heated pan needs to be shimmeringly hot.
- **If it all gets a bit much, take a deep breath and reread the recipe.** Unlike in my '10 minutes to table' videos (www.telegraph.co.uk/food), you don't (I hope) have a stopwatch ticking away, so it doesn't matter if it takes a few minutes longer. Speed comes with practice.

The kitchen speedway: how to have a kitchen that helps you cook fast

- **Do get tough on clutter.** You need space to cook efficiently, but few of us have a huge kitchen. Keep whatever kitchen surfaces you have clear, so anything kept out has to earn its place. Lose anything that's purely decorative and put away any jars, bottles or equipment that isn't used at least once a day.
- **Do clear your cupboards** of out-of-date ingredients, and be realistic, get rid of equipment you are never going to use. Take it to a local charity shop or recycle on www.freecycle.org (where you can also pass on unwanted and unloved, but still in date, ingredients).
- **Do use a rack** or hanging rail to hang your favourite kitchen tools, the ones that are used (and washed) at least twice a week.
- **Don't leave out things you only use occasionally:** kitchen air is inevitably full of grease and fumes, and they'll get covered in sticky dust.
- **Do put up narrow shelves** (say 15cm/6 inches) at eye level for the ingredients and equipment that you use frequently.
- **Don't get deep shelves if possible,** stuff gets lost and hidden at the back.

A few rule of thumb measurements: easy conversions

- **Don't get too hung up with quantities.** None of the recipes in this book will fail because you have an ounce more or less of any ingredient.
- **That said, for the flatbreads, tortillas and pasta,** some sort of measurement will help. This is where the American cup system, relying on volume rather than weight, is useful. The scoop-and-fill method is perfect for quick suppers.
- **A normal teacup is fine for a cup measure** (check how much it holds by filling it with water, then pouring the water into a measuring jug), or invest in a standard American cup measure. It is best to use a proper tablespoon measure though.

- **1 teacupful** = 8fl oz = 225ml = 110g (4oz) flour = 225g (8oz) sugar
- **Liquids:** 1 tbsp = 15ml = ½fl oz
- **Butter:** 1 level tbsp = 15g (½oz)
- **Flour:** 1 rounded tbsp = 15g (½oz)   1 teeteringly high, heaped dsp = 30g (1oz)
- **Couscous:** ½ teacupful of couscous soaked in ½ teacupful of boiling water = 1 serving (always use equal volumes of liquid and couscous)
- **Polenta:** ¼ teacupful of quick-cook '1 minute' polenta cooked with 1 teacupful of boiling water = 1 serving (always use four times the volume of liquid to polenta)

index

Anchovies
  Salmon, anchovy butter and new
    potatoes 92
  Spinach with pine nuts and
    raisins 152
apples: Pork with apple and
  Calvados sauce 31
artichokes
  Crisp chicken with yoghurt dip
    and a winter salad 78
  Seared tuna with artichokes 103
asparagus
  Asparagus with mozzarella,
    pine nuts and peas 136
  Asparagus with poached duck
    egg and Parmesan wafers 139
avocados
  Ceviche of salmon with
    avocado and red onion 128
  Club sandwich 85
Bacon
  Chicken with garlic cream
    cheese sauce 63
  Club sandwich 85
  Lentils with bacon 49
  Little courgette pancakes 156
  Warm salad of baby spinach,
    chicken livers and bacon 74
beans
  English salade niçoise 105
  Haricot beans with chorizo 29
  Homemade tortillas with
    guacamole 164
  Lamb cutlets with salsa verde
    and haricot beans 51

Polenta with green beans 24
Salmon with pesto and
  prosciutto 116
Saltimbocca with green beans 22
Seared tuna with beans 103
Spring lamb with braised little
  gems and Jersey Royals 46
Bruschetta of haricot beans,
  lemon and chilli 169
Tuscan bean soup 168
beef
  Parmesan beef burger and
    chips 13
  'Phast pho' 34
  Rare beef with radish, cress
    and pea salad 14
  Steak au poivre with parsnip
    chips 18
beetroot
  Beetroot soup with horseradish
    cream 161
  Calves' liver alla veneziana 21
bread
  Chicken Caesar salad with
    homemade garlic croûtons 71
  Club sandwich 85
  Crab cakes 109
  Homemade flatbread 66
  Mezze with homemade thyme
    flatbread 155
  Pappardelle with mushrooms,
    and lemon crumbs 161
broccoli
  Edamame peas with soy, broccoli
    and noodles 150

Salmon, purple-sprouting
  broccoli and new potatoes 92
Smoked haddock with Puy lentils
  and citrus broccoli 124
Carrots
  Duck breast with soft polenta
    and caramelized carrots 83
  Thai turkey nam jim 86
  Thick cut ham with buttery
    carrots and a mustard cream 48
  Tuscan bean soup 168
cheese
  Asparagus with mozzarella 136
  Asparagus with poached duck
    egg and Parmesan wafers 139
  Cheese and chorizo quesadillas 35
  Chicken with garlic cream
    cheese sauce 63
  Couscous with harissa, rocket
    and goats' cheese 153
  Figs with mozzarella 41
  Parmesan beef burger 13
  Parmesan chicken 567
  Pea and herb frittata with a
    goats' cheese cream 149
  Smoky cheese fondue 170
  Soft polenta with prosciutto 24
  Spinach Parmesan pancakes 120
  Tomato, soft cheese and sesame
    tart 140
chicken
  Chicken Caesar salad 71
  Chicken noodle soup 61
  Chicken, pak choi and almond
    stir-fry 59

index

Chicken with garlic cream cheese sauce 63
Cold chicken, dill, mint and rocket salad 73
Crisp chicken with herb yoghurt dip and a winter salad 78
Green chicken curry 76
Chicken with cardamom 66
Parmesan chicken 56
Smoked chicken with pecans 84
Tom yam soup 108
Warm salad of baby spinach, chicken livers and bacon 74
clams: Vermicelli con vongole 94
cod: Crisp fish with minted mushy peas 100
courgettes
  Green chicken curry 76
  Lamb kofta skewers with grilled tomatoes and courgettes 42
  Little courgette pancakes 156
  Parmesan chicken, courgettes and fresh tomato sauce 56
  Ricotta, spring vegetables and tarragon pasta 160
couscous
  Couscous with harissa, rocket and goats' cheese 153
  Harissa mackerel with mint couscous 110
  Mezze with homemade thyme flatbread 155
Duck
  Duck breast with soft polenta and caramelized carrots 83
  Noodles with teriyaki sauce and smoked duck 62
Eggs
  Asparagus with poached duck egg and Parmesan wafers 139
  English salade niçoise 105
  Huevos revueltos 40
Figs with mozzarella, Parma ham and breadsticks 41
fish, see individual names of fish
Haddock
  Smoked haddock with crème fraîche and chives 124
  Spinach and Parmesan pancakes with smoked haddock 120
ham
  Figs with mozzarella, Parma ham and breadsticks 41
  Polenta with prosciutto 24
  Salmon with pesto and prosciutto 116
  Saltimbocca with green beans 22
  Thick cut ham 48
Lamb
  Lamb cutlets with salsa verde 51
  Lamb kofta skewers 42
  Spring lamb with braised little gems and Jersey Royals 46
lentils
  Lentils with bacon 49
  Seared tuna with lime lentils 131
  Smoked haddock with crème fraîche and Puy lentils 124
Mackerel: Harissa mackerel with mint couscous 110

mushrooms: Pappardelle with mushrooms 163
Mussels with coconut, chilli and lemon grass 126
mustard
  Mustard, honey and thyme quail with rosemary potatoes 64
  Pork with sweet potato mash and mustard sauce 26
  Thick cut ham with buttery carrots and a mustard cream 48
Noodles
  Chicken noodle soup 61
  Edamame peas with noodles 150
  Noodles with teriyaki sauce and smoked duck 62
Parsnips: parsnip chips 18
pasta
  Homemade pasta with garlic, chilli and rocket 158
  Ricotta, spring vegetables and tarragon pasta 160
peas
  Crisp fish with minted mushy peas 100
  Edamame peas with noodles 150
  English salade niçoise 105
  Pea and herb frittata 149
  Pea and mint soup 145
  Rare beef with pea salad 14
  Ricotta, spring vegetables and tarragon pasta 160
  Spring lamb with peas and Jersey Royals 46
plaice: Fillet of with capers 102
polenta
  Chipolatas with polenta 36
  Duck breast with soft polenta 83
  Polenta with prosciutto 24
  Rose veal with thyme-scented polenta and spinach 16
  Saltimbocca with green beans, polenta and Marsala gravy 22
pork
  Butternut squash, chorizo and prawns 39
  Cheese and chorizo quesadillas 35
  Chipolatas with red onion gravy 36
  Haricot beans with chorizo 29
  Huevos revueltos 40
  Pork with apple and Calvados 31
  Pork with sweet potato mash 26
potatoes
  Asparagus with mozzarella and new potatoes 136
  English salade niçoise 105
  Fresh sardines with Jersey Royals 96
  Mustard, honey and thyme quail with rosemary potatoes 64
  Pan-fried rainbow trout with pink fir apple potatoes 106
  Parmesan burger with chips 13
  Pork with apple and watercress crushed potatoes 31
  Salmon and new potatoes 92
  Sea trout with horseradish potatoes 115
  Spring lamb with braised little gems and Jersey Royals 46

prawns
  Butternut squash, chorizo and prawns 39
  Speedy fish soup 118
  Tom yam soup 108
Quail: Mustard, honey and thyme quail with rosemary potatoes 64
Salmon
  Ceviche of salmon with avocado and red onion 128
  Salmon, purple-sprouting broccoli and new potatoes 92
  Salmon with pesto and prosciutto 116
  Smoked salmon chowder 129
  Speedy fish soup 118
sardines: Fresh sardines with Jersey Royals 96
scallops: with Sauce vierge 95
spinach
  Chipolatas with wilted garlic spinach 36
  Pan-fried rainbow trout with lemon and garlic spinach 106
  Rose veal with spinach 16
  Spinach and Parmesan pancakes with smoked haddock 120
  Spinach with pine nuts and raisins 152
  Warm salad of baby spinach, chicken livers and bacon 74
squid: Salt and pepper squid 112
Tomatoes
  Beetroot soup with horseradish cream 161
  Gazpacho with olive and goats' cheese toasts 146
  Huevos revueltos 40
  Lamb cutlets with salsa verde and blackened tomatoes 51
  Lamb kofta skewers with grilled tomatoes and hummus 42
  Mezze with homemade thyme flatbread 155
  Parmesan beef burger with tomato and balsamic relish 13
  Parmesan chicken and fresh tomato sauce 56
  Pea and herb frittata with tomato salad 149
  Rose veal with cherry tomato sauce and spinach 16
  Tomato and soft cheese tart 140
trout
  Pan-fried rainbow trout 106
  Sea trout 115
tuna
  English salade niçoise 105
  Seared tuna with beans and artichokes 103
  Seared tuna with lime lentils and a soy dipping sauce 131
turkey
  Club sandwich 85
  Thai turkey nam jim 86
Veal
  Rose veal with thyme-scented polenta and spinach 16
  Saltimbocca with green beans, polenta and Marsala gravy 22